Sunny Side Up

Sunny Side Up

*A Memoir of a
Young Woman's
Search for
Transformation*

BJ Appelgren

Acknowledgements

To Bruce for his unquestioning support, my Read and Critique writing teachers Tara Bell, Kathryn Cobb, Millie Curtis, Pam Miller, Karen Robinson, and Priscilla Rodd, and my fellow journeymen.

Published by Zillah, Inc.

Library of Congress Control Number 2012932907

ISBN 978-0-961-9884-2-5

Printed in the United States of America.

Cover illustration by Molly Goldstein based on lost art done at Sherborne House by BJ Appelgren called *Freshly Laundered and Hanging Out to Dry.*

CONTENTS

FOREWORD

Sunny Side Up is a description of my experience at a school called Sherborne House, sponsored by the International Academy for Continuous Education. John G. Bennett was the principal and the one hundred and three students there that year, whose age ranged from seventeen to seventy-something, chose to be there because of what they had heard of his philosophy, which promised the practical application and continuous development of man's bodily, mental, and spiritual powers.

The names of living people or those whose status is unknown to me have been changed to provide anonymity.

I

INTRODUCTION

1 ∾ GARDENING WITH CUTLERY

The present is what it is, but it may be possible to change the future. We can only reap now the harvest sown in the past, and if we feel compassion for the sufferings of the present and we wish a different harvest for those who are to come, we must sow different seeds now.

JG Bennett

It is early spring 1973. I am using a dessertspoon to dig dandelions out from the great lawn. We're in front of Sherborne House, a nineteenth century manor turned into an experimental spiritual school for adults in the village of Sherborne, Gloucestershire, England. One hundred and two other warm bodies are out here with me, silently doing the same thing. Well, not everyone is using a dessertspoon. The people who arrived first got garden tools and the rest of us procured cutlery from the dining hall. We've learned to creatively make do with what we have. It's one of the many lessons we're learning.

Every fifteen minutes someone rings a bell which signals us to become even more still, to sense the next point on the body according to a pattern we've been taught of moving our attention through sixty points starting at the top of the head, going down the left side and up the right, perhaps to breathe into the point, perhaps to say some words that help us blend energies of sensation and intention.

Having been here for months, I nevertheless keep forgetting to do the exercise. It's as if I've used up any internal storage space I might have had for making such efforts. Mostly I just do from the outside what we've been given to do and depend on the actions of others—standing still, looking attentive—to remind me of that much.

As I end the lives of dandelions I have no wish to kill, I see four-year old me tugging at my mother's skirt while she chats with a neighbor. They're standing on the lawn behind our house seemingly oblivious to my presence. Finally, mother notes my tugs and bends over to hear what I'm trying to whisper. I do not want to embarrass my mother's friend so I ask Mom to move the lady off the dandelion she is stepping on. My mother tells her and they both have a good laugh.

I notice again that we students are on the lawn hoping our efforts will allow something higher to enter into us. Am I grateful to love everyone here with me or am I more grateful to understand that I don't have to live this way forever?

The knees of my dungarees are soaking wet from the dew that is still on the grass despite a welcome sunny day. I've long become used to such discomforts and inner confusion, though only occasionally do I think about how I got here, how badly I wanted to be here, joking with my friends about going to a monastery. Not that it is a monastery. At least, J.G. Bennett, the draftsman of the experiment never called it that. He called it a course. On the other hand, maybe it is a monastery in the traditional sense of the word—a community of people living together for spiritual purposes—though in this case, only for a ten-month period of study.

NOT THAT THE STORY NEED BE LONG,
BUT IT WILL TAKE A LONG WHILE TO MAKE IT SHORT.

Henry David Thoreau

Two years before, life conspired to send me on a more active search for a meaningful existence. I had always tended toward depression, and although I was doing much better, the free-lance design and part-time teaching jobs in Chicago didn't speak to my hunger for meaning. Then, after taking a full-time job as a graphic designer, a never-ending schedule of expensive redecoration and furniture replacements alerted us to the fact that our company was an orchestrated tax write-off for the umbrella corporation that owned it. They never intended to complete the business school franchises we were working on; thus explaining the glacial speed at which the higher-ups approved our work.

At the same time, my roommate and I were informed that the three-story apartment building we lived in with marble halls and wainscoted walls was about to be torn down. A blocky, twenty-story skyscraper was going to replace it along with the dark brick apartment building next door. We were living in one of the last Victorian jewels in a prime location near the lake and Lincoln Park. Christine, whom I loved living with, decided it was time anyway to strike out on her own.

IF YOU COME TO A FORK IN THE ROAD, TAKE IT.

Yogi Berra

Growing up in Chicago, schoolmates in my neighborhood were mostly first-generation Americans—Swedish Lutheran, Irish Catholic, and Russian Jewish—all trying to assimilate into the American dream.

While many of our parents had not even finished high school, I was part of the first generation to attend an unprecedented thirteen years of school paid for by the government. In 1966, by the time I earned a master's degree from the venerable Art Institute of Chicago, a growing feeling of civil dissatisfaction was hovering in the air.

Despite democratic ideals we'd studied for so many years, Jim Crow laws were still well established. Blacks were kept from voting, and, most horrific of all, still being lynched. We were learning that our country used more than its share of natural resources, often taken at unfair rates from poorer countries. No credence was given to sustainable forms of energy production even though problems with the economics and supply of petroleum were well recognized. Corporations were dictating political decisions, including our involvement in a war in Viet Nam.

All I wanted was for America to live up to our democratic principles. Imagine my generation's befuddlement when parents and mentors became incensed over a wish to correct the country that had given us so much. Weren't we all working for progress and didn't progress mean making changes to benefit the majority of people on the planet—even if it required giving up some of our personal advantages? It's what we were taught in school and our religions. Many of my friends and acquaintances felt resigned, saying that's just the way things are. You can't fight city hall.

For years, I seemed to be the only one in my neighborhood to think we should be able to reduce inequities and prevent further destruction to the environment. But in graduate school I heard more reactions similar to mine, full of longing. We shared a conviction that we didn't *have to* live this way— unfair to minorities, focused on money and material possessions. For the first time, there was a sense of hope that positive change could happen.

The press referred to us as flower children, considered little more than misguided youngsters making a rebellious fashion statement. Experimentation with drugs was described as a new form of self-indulgent inebriation, not seen by society as a hunger for the ephemeral world of spirit. After much personal agony and guidance from a dead friend in a dream, travelling around Europe to explore life's possibilities became my chosen preoccupation.

I hadn't thought of myself as a hippie. Weren't *they* political activists? But while wandering Europe and the near East that's what people called me. In 1970, who else would travel for seven months without an itinerary, carrying only a backpack, not even knowing if she were going to return home? Who else but a young American had the wealth and freedom to do that?

By selling a few pieces of furniture, dozens of houseplants, and much of my artwork, I raised $3000, enough to travel reasonably for months. My Jewish family couldn't speak with me about going to Europe. The reality of WWII was not history to *them*. None of my friends were willing to go with me, yet when I embarked on the lonely journey, my doubts were soothed to some degree by meeting droves of Americans in Europe who were my age and doing the same thing—searching. I hadn't expected that. We came upon spiritual avenues, too, not intentionally at first—being invited to meditate, learning about Eastern religions accidentally, then being touched by the serenity of those experiences in ways we didn't know we yearned for.

I was bursting with the revelations of my wanderings: one, Travel was scary unless I was accompanied by people who went with me to the next destination; two, People actually talked to me when I didn't have my clever artwork nearby, which I thought of as props; and three, I loved the spontaneous 'group' experiences of cooking, learning about different cultures and landscapes, even defecating together, like when we traveled as a group to camp out on the land. We rented a communal cottage in Epano Zakros, a pristine Greek beach village and took hotel rooms in the slums of exotic cities like Istanbul or Tehran.

I returned to Chicago after seven months of travel still wondering if the differences among human beings just couldn't be reconciled. Couldn't we at least agree to live peacefully? I thought that's what a spiritual life was all about. Yet, underneath the logic was another motivator many of us shared—a growing feeling of urgency that the material excesses of our culture would suddenly catch up with us, that the disharmony of our exploits might even contribute to earth changes. Our lumbering institutions would not be able to respond in a timely way to large-scale catastrophe, whether, economic, social, or environmental. I didn't know how I'd become so concerned about these things when the people I grew up with were not.

I worked a few freelance jobs, lived with my old roommate again in her new apartment, took meditation-related workshops, but still had no sense of where I belonged in the world. Nevertheless, at the forefront of my thoughts were my persistent mystical longings.

During this time, my mother invited me to go to England on a ten-day trip with her and her sister, my Aunt Mary. Some days I wandered through London on my own and other days joined them on bus tours out of the city. The sites we visited— stone circles and Stonehenge, Stratford, Winchester Cathedral— all had a magical and familiar feeling.

On the flight home, Aunt Mary asked me, "Hadn't you been to England on your long trip last year?"

"No. I'd meant to but it always seemed out of the way." Then I added, with no specific intention, "You know, after all these travels, England is the only country I have an interest in returning to." But I had no immediate reason for doing so and was still exploring Chicago for meaningful activities.

HUMANS CANNOT COME TO TRUTH THROUGH ANY ORGANIZA-
TION, THROUGH ANY CREED, THROUGH ANY DOGMA, PRIEST,
OR RITUAL, NOT THROUGH ANY PHILOSOPHIC KNOWLEDGE
OR PSYCHOLOGICAL TECHNIQUE. THEY HAVE TO FIND IT
THROUGH THE UNDERSTANDING OF THE CONTENTS OF THEIR
OWN MINDS, THROUGH OBSERVATION AND NOT THROUGH
INTELLECTUAL ANALYSIS OR INTROSPECTIVE DISSECTION.

J. Krishnamurti

I practiced a meditation that I'd learned at an Edgar Cayce Foundation retreat a couple of years before. Cayce, who died in

1945, was a clairvoyant whose work was documented by 14,000 transcriptions of psychic health readings he gave, many for people he never met. Many of his diagnoses were later confirmed by health professionals. He became famous for introducing terms like meditation, akashic records, spiritual growth, auras, and holism into our vocabulary. His suggestions for health care made him one of the first in contemporary times to describe a holistic and preventative approach.

I also often attended various workshops at Oasis, a local center that sponsored seminars led by well-known teachers of human potential such as Lama Govinda and Joseph Campbell. At a two-day introduction to Buddhist meditation, I met Robin, a sprite-like man with a reddish beard. Between his casual plaid shirt and relaxed attitude, he seemed like someone to confide in.

"I wish there were a study group I could continue meditating with."

He looked at me, as if making a decision. Then he said, "I teach a class called *Varieties of Religious Experience* at the Theological Union. I'm a Jesuit priest. We meditate during part of each class. If you were my assistant, you could participate."

So I signed on wondering what the odds were of a Jewish girl being made that offer. Along with meditation, we studied an ancient system of nine ego fixations represented on a figure called the enneagram. The symbol's origins dated back to Pythagoras or possibly spiritual schools in the Caucasus. Understanding the fixations was supposed to help us learn to transcend the particular sufferings caused by our mechanistic behavior patterns.

In addition, we read Middle Eastern teaching stories transmitted by a contemporary Afghan, Idries Shah. Many of

the stories were familiar to me in the form of jokes or their simi-
larity to Gracie Allen's quirky perspective on life, but their main
intent was, once again, to show patterns of human behavior,
interaction, and points of view.

After class, several weeks into the course, Robin handed
me a book. It was thick and well worn, the hardcover fabric
an uneven faded blue. "I think you'll find this interesting," he
said. "It's J. G. Bennett's autobiography, *Witness*. He's a philosopher, eclectic in a way that reminds me of how you think about
things." I took it, more curious to see what Robin thought was
my way of thinking than to read the autobiography of a philosopher I'd never heard of.

I finished it before the next meeting. Robin had been correct
about my feeling a kinship. Central to my interest was Bennett's
conviction that there is a common spiritual foundation underlying all religious paths. I'd never heard any authority say that before.

GOD IS TOO BIG TO FIT INTO ONE RELIGION.

Robert A. Heinlein

In *Witness*, Bennett also wrote about his gifts with language and
the persistence he applied to learning in regards to his spiritual life. He sounded evenhanded because he also addressed his
weaknesses, pointing out, especially, his slow comprehension of
emotional circumstances.

I didn't understand the degree to which Bennett devoted
his life to his philosophical writings about a unified theory of
energies from mechanical to cosmic, or how he understood
human life to fit into the universal scheme of energies. Nor did

I have a clear picture of the methods he researched to aid the students he taught. He discussed sacred dances called Movements, assorted meditations, prayers and exercises that came from different spiritual traditions, and a few mystical experiences he'd had while studying with his teachers.

Reading about his spiritual journey had me entertaining a fresh thought: "Now here's someone who would have been interesting to study with." Even in art school, the idea of studying with an admired artist had never occurred to me. Judging by the dates of events in Bennett's life, I assumed he was no longer alive. However, at Robin's next class, he handed me a brochure. It was the Prospectus of the International Academy for Continuous Education, a new ten-month program Mr. Bennett was holding at a place called Sherborne House. He *was* alive . . . and taking students! Robin was corresponding with him. The school was located in the Cotswolds, just below a region in England known as West Midlands, an interesting twist on where I lived—the Midwest, Chicagoland, as we referred to it. Mr. Bennett's birthday was the same as mine, and these little coincidences caught my attention, making them feel important.

On the cover of the Prospectus was a somewhat fuzzy picture of an English manor with barren trees, their long shadows in the foreground indicating winter. Within the booklet was a riveting photo of students wearing loose white tunics over baggy white pants gathered at the ankles—costumes worn for public demonstrations of Movements. The dancers were barefoot, standing in postures that reminded me, with my background in art, of ancient temple sculptures. Bennett's first course of the five that he intended to preside over was already in progress.

On the first page of the prospectus, it said that it was addressed to people who care about the future . . . "especially to those who have already searched and experimented with politics, social service, those who have looked for new experience in travel, in sex or in drugs, for those who have tried religion or plunged into one of the many 'isms' and movements that promise a new world, and have found them all lacking in an essential ingredient: that is practicality. . . . It is particularly directed to those who are acutely aware of an unrealized self, of energies squandered and of time wasted—who are prepared to go through a hard training in order to change. It is above all, for those who have realized that the 'first step in helping the world is to help oneself,' that inner change must come before outer change."

How could I not think it was addressed to me? I hadn't known it, but this was the kind of information I'd been searching for.

As I held the prospectus in my hands, my mind racing to take it all in, I heard my voice say to Robin, "I'm going there."

ALL HUMAN BEINGS SHOULD TRY TO LEARN BEFORE THEY DIE,
WHAT THEY ARE RUNNING FROM,
AND TO, AND WHY.

James Thurber

2 ❧ OFF TO THE COURSE

There is a general lack of faith among people that transformation is possible. If we have no faith, we have no force, and therefore we have to recognize that we have to begin without force, because faith only comes in the course of the process of transformation.

JG Bennett

It's mid-September 1972, and once again I'm on a venture my parents don't approve of. As my plane leaves New York, I stare anxiously out the window. Images of the friends I'm leaving behind and questions I have about how we will create a more just society consume me. Although most of the flight is during the night, it doesn't look as if I'm going to be getting much sleep. I'm too excited and have begun worrying about finding my way to the school. Is the train station near the airport? Will a cab driver be willing to drive to a school far into the countryside? In addition, flashes of sheet lightning in the night sky cause me to brace my body against expected turbulence. Maybe we'll never make it to England. The ride remains smooth, however, and, finally overhearing some passengers talking, I learn that the ominous green flickering curtains are the northern lights.

I manage to catch a few naps and, shortly after daybreak, revive with a second wind. At London's Heathrow Airport, signs lead me right to the train for the next part of my journey. Liberation from that worry, however, reinstates my sleepiness. Now I put my remaining energy into fighting the hypnotic rhythm of the railway. I don't want to miss the station where I have to change trains. At Reading, I strain my back lugging the oversized yellow leather suitcase down the stairs from one platform and up the stairs to another. Only stewardesses have those new suitcases on wheels. I'm full of regret for having packed a load of books. Did I really think there'd be time to read or that they didn't sell books in England? I must have felt they'd be comforting.

At Cheltenham, I take a taxi the last seventeen miles, exhausted and sore by mid-afternoon when I arrive at Sherborne House. After wistfully watching the cab drive off, I turn my attention to the building . . . and shudder. It has a looming presence—stone, three stories high, half a city block long, squat in a bulldog-ish way I recognize only in English architecture. The coarse gravel scattered on the ground spreads in disarray from the driveway to the front entrance, a crude contrast to the surrounding immaculate green hills, punctuated with perfectly grouped trees.

Although it is mid-September, a drop of temperature inside the building sets a chill rattling up my spine, raising the hairs on my bare arms. Standing just inside the doorway, I hesitate, wondering whether to call out or to start searching for someone. Then I hear a rising crescendo of echoing footsteps that eventually produces a young man. He happens to be walking through this part of the house. He greets me with concern, and learning I'm a new student, he runs off to fetch someone named Mick. A moment later, a handsome pale skinned Englishman in his early thirties, just a couple of years older than I, arrives. He has almost black hair and sparkling dark eyes. A navy sports coat combined with Levis and a silk cravat at the neck of his white shirt gives him a casual yet elegant air. Talking and smiling, Mick leads me through the cavernous unfurnished room nearest the entrance. A tall vase of freshly cut flowers stands on the floor next to the fireplace. The architectural details include cream-colored pillars, fireplace, moldings, and a polished Cotswold marble floor.

"In this room on visitors' weekends, we sometimes perform Movements," he explains, "and serve tea up on the landing." There, too, is a vase of fresh flowers on a table. Then, turning to me, he asks, "How are you doing—tired?"

"Yeah, I'm so cold. I need to get another layer of clothing on."

Mick smiles. "Have you been in England long?"

"I just flew overnight from visiting my parents in Chicago. Before that, I'd been in Virginia Beach on a six-week meditation course with the Edgar Cayce Foundation. They're experimenting with the idea of starting a university. Do you know them?"

"Oh, yes, I've heard of them. I think you'll find this a bit different, more intense, I suspect. Would you like to rest?"

Instead of saying, 'Oh, god, would I ever!' I tell him, "I'd rather *do* something in order to get acclimated to the time change."

Mick smiles, again. "Well, there's always plenty of work. Why don't we get you settled in first? You'll soon enough be sick and tired of tasks, so before sweeping the upstairs hall, let me show you to your room." Spirited as he is, I keep feeling he's laughing at my answers to his friendly questions.

I breathe a sigh of gratitude when without hesitation he grabs my bag and carries it up two floors for me. "The daily schedule of assignments is posted here," he says, pointing to the bulletin board we pass at the top of the grand staircase. "Of course, you won't be on today's list.

"The day begins with a Morning Exercise, a meditation, at 6:45 and ends with Movements from 8:30-10 p.m. You won't be expected to attend Movements until the course begins. Right now, they're just for the first year students who stayed on to help during the two-month transition between courses. Tomorrow you can attend Morning Exercise, though, and just sit without doing an inner exercise."

My dorm is on the third floor, 'the second floor up' as the English would say, once maids' quarters, with low ceilings. As Mick escorts me into the austere room I notice that there's no form of heat but a barren fireplace. Two shards of tile are all that remain from what once must have been an elegant ceramic liner.

Mick suggests I come find him near the kitchen when I've gotten settled in. "It's on the ground floor. Just follow the sound of voices and clanking pans," he says over his shoulder as he leaves.

I sit down on one of the beds Mick said was available, perhaps attracted to the warm glow of its orange blanket, glad to finally catch my breath and take in the new surroundings. The walls are devoid of decoration. No curtains or rugs. A half dozen narrow cots are placed square to the walls and each other throughout the room, thin mattresses on mesh springs, the unoccupied ones having a neat stack of their appointed sheets, wool blankets, pillows, and down afghans. A couple of suitcases and made-up beds indicate that at least two other occupants are somewhere around.

It feels good to stow away my clothing into a deep drawer chosen from among the unmatched chests. The books remain in my suitcase under the bed. After making up the spare-looking cot, I lay down, sinking into exhaustion. The thought of remaining motionless in the cold, however, is too crushing. Even if I manage to bundle up enough, I'd probably sleep only into the middle of the night. Then what would I do? Now that I'm finally here, I can't allow myself to rest; my inner motor is revving.

There are two months between each of the intended ten-month courses. First course students were invited to stay after theirs and second course students were offered the opportunity to arrive early at no extra cost to ease the school's transition between student bodies. I am here a month early, thinking to ease myself into the foreign environment where I know no one. Students run the house and care for the property along with staff, so if we don't know how to cook, clean, garden, or repair things, we will learn through doing. We are to take turns with every role, even house supervisor, the student who makes the work assignments for the day and will oversee all practical activity.

Mick and I didn't pass a soul in the halls on the way to the dorm and the starkness here hints at desolation. Every now and then, I hear voices coming from far away. I need to find them and push away the gnawing emptiness that has nothing to do with food.

THERE ARE MANY WAYS OF GOING FORWARD,
BUT ONLY ONE WAY OF STANDING STILL.

Franklin D. Roosevelt

3 ❧ TRANSITION

Every one of us has weaknesses that we have inherited from parents and grandparents, and so on. We have to accept this and by overcoming those weaknesses in ourselves, we liberate both past and future generations. In that way we can break the line of transmission.

JG Bennett

I have no trouble finding Mick when I'm ready. It's as if he pops into existence when needed. After we visit the broom closet, he starts me sweeping a wide, seemingly endless hallway that runs the full length of the first floor up—a tedious task when I'm feeling so tired and the floor looks so clean.

Mick shows up again just when I arrive at the turn of the corridor, where a deep paneled wooden door, maybe twice the height of an ordinary one, stands ajar.

"Come here," he says, crooking his finger. He opens the door fully to reveal an elegant ballroom with a sparkling crystal chandelier, plaster swags along the top of panel moldings on several walls, a grand piano at the far end, and an expansive hardwood floor. Also, bewildering to see in that baroque room, are three six-by-fifteen foot expressionist paintings hanging on the long wall next to the entrance door. They're more like graphic designs with bold strokes. Two have deep magenta backgrounds and one has a deep green background. The black brush strokes suggest energized movement yet also convey a sense of balance.

"This is the room where we do Morning Exercise, the morning meditation," Mick tells me. "Most of the Movements classes are in here, too."

What he really wants to show me, though, having learned that I'm an artist, is the superb craftsmanship of the solid wood door that led us into the room. We return to it, standing outside the room once again.

"It must weigh hundreds of pounds." With reverence, he points out, "Look how perfectly it's set on its hinges." Then, with his index finger, he gives the massive door a gentle push, sending it soundlessly toward the jamb until the hardware clicks into place. We both stare at it in dumb admiration. Perhaps he shares with me the notion that craftsmanship provides clues about the Great Creator.

Over the next few days, I become familiar with the estate, my home for the next eleven months. Having grown up in Chicago, one of my initial worries at Sherborne is about the door to the building being left unlocked at all times. Images of *Chicago Tribune* headlines haunt me, ones about an unknown killer sauntering into a government official's home in the middle of the night and suffocating his twenty-one-year-old daughter with a pillow. My only solace to worrying is the fact that my room is two floors up. Here I am sleeping in a house with sixty strangers and fretting about the possibility of other strangers walking in on us. After several restless nights fighting off visions of murder and mayhem, sheer exhaustion finally banishes the issue.

Throughout the day we follow the same schedule that will be used once school begins, though I am given to understand that what is referred to as the current informality will soon be replaced with demanding and mostly silent intensity.

Each day, new work assignments introduce me to a few more members of the sparse yet ever present population. I am told there are about sixty people here but the house and grounds are so generous I hardly ever see more than a few at a time except in the garden and at meals.

Ten to twenty of us pull weeds amidst the vegetables, three or four help the cook by washing or cutting vegetables, one or two clean pots and utensils as meals are being prepared and then wash more cooking vessels after the meal. Maybe four people serve food and wash dishes and the stainless tableware after meals. Additional practical work includes washing and ironing sheets, painting rooms, patching walls, sweeping floors, and scraping the old finish off of wood trim.

Everyone also helps feed and care for sheep, a horse, two donkeys, and chickens from which we collect 50-60 eggs a day. Another part of our work is maintaining the buildings and grounds. One minute a person can be glazing windows and, the next, putting up beets for the winter. I love the idea of so many practical activities, looking forward to them with relish. It is, at least in part, a reaction to having done so much rote work in school.

When I meet other students, I am greeted with a smile and friendly conversation, usually about where we come from. There are as many Americans as Brits plus a few students from Australia, New Zealand, Sweden, Ireland, and Germany.

Sometimes when I walk down a hall or garden path, when the purpose of my activity isn't apparent, people whom I assume are staff members bark at me.

"Where are you going?"

"What are you doing?"

Unlike Mick, they are unsmiling. Why are they so grouchy? They bring to mind scenes with the Queen of Hearts from *Alice in Wonderland*. I learn that in some cases they are first-year students who take it upon themselves to police newcomers, intent on rescuing us from developing bad habits.

I HAVE AN EXISTENTIAL MAP.
IT HAS 'YOU ARE HERE' WRITTEN ALL OVER IT.

Steven Wright

One afternoon, Mick is showing me where I should harvest spinach for dinner. While we're out there he takes me on a tour of the gardens, pointing out how everything is still in fruition. "Beans. Radishes. Potatoes. Herbs. We've eaten plenty, but there's still a lot more to harvest. The weather is mild enough that we'll be able to eat spinach and kale through most of the winter," he says.

We neophytes are inheriting the bounty of the previous students' work before contributing anything ourselves. The more I think about it, the more I realize how this is true in most aspects of life, but I have never before been so aware of it.

Once I'm familiar with the garden, when I need a moment by myself, I skip tea or spend the end of lunch hour there for visual nourishment. It is a fairyland of shiny-leafed knee-high spinach, white-stalked Swiss chard, claret-stemmed beets, red-caned rhubarb with leaves the size of elephant ears, squashes of all shapes and colors, the vegetables as beautiful as the flowers which grow tumbling among them and along a garden wall. At meals, simple as most of them are, I am reminded of what I'd often heard but never before experienced, that fresh food tastes exceptional.

On my forays, I notice the beginnings of a rock garden and look forward to a time when I'll have the opportunity to work on it. Meanwhile, I manage in spare moments to rescue potted plants that have been abandoned in various parts of the house and organize them in a bright spot in one of the hallways. Securing from the kitchen an empty glass gallon jar that once held mayonnaise, I create a terrarium to add to the hallway garden, and include in it some ferns that Mick had pointed out. They seem very exotic to me though they grow all over England's stone walls. I also collect some grasses and flowers that are drying in the fields, making decorative bouquets to cheer us when the flowers are no longer blooming. My childhood didn't include much conversation, and despite growing up in the city, I learned to enjoy the company of plants in our tiny backyard.

Despite thinking of myself as a social person and knowing that only about half the students are here yet, occupying myself with the plants is comforting. I'm discovering that my optimism for the promise of Sherborne doesn't quite counteract feeling overwhelmed by the long days, constant companionship, and a paradoxical sense of isolation.

Mick invites me to help him gather squashes. "These are marrows for dinner tonight," he says, indicating some pale green ones as large as serving platters. Licking his lips, he describes how he's going to prepare them. Everything he mentions seems to be great fun he looks forward to. "I'll cut them in half, stuff them with a tangy meat and vegetable mixture, and then bake them." His enthusiasm starts me salivating for dinner.

Before heading back to cook anything, however, he suggests collecting a display of more colorful inedible gourds. "We're giving these to a local church as decoration for their harvest festival. How about making the quick drive with me to deliver them?"

This little outing off the property feels like a great treat. I eagerly follow him to the car and walk into his backside when he halts at the right-hand car door. Realizing I'm not used to the reversed driving sides, Mick directs me to the passenger seat on the left.

YOU CAN DISCOVER MORE ABOUT A PERSON IN AN
HOUR OF PLAY THAN IN A YEAR OF CONVERSATION.

Plato

On Saturday night, Mick, almost dancing, leads a laughing group of us on a path through the woods, probably not more than a quarter of a mile long, over to the local Social Club in nearby Sherborne village. The town of Sherborne is a dead ringer for old illustrations I've seen in children's books. Having always thought they were fantasy pictures of fairy dwellings, now I understand that they had been realistic renderings of Cotswold villages. Lining the street are little stone row houses with peaked roofs of slate or an occasional rounded one of thatch, walls covered with ivy, flower gardens instead of front lawns, and flowers cascading from window boxes. Thick grass or mowed chamomile paths look like shag carpeting leading to the front doors or around the side to backyard gardens.

Because the Social Club is a private membership pub, children are allowed. For a nominal annual fee of one pound, whole families come to watch TV and play games: chess, checkers, cards, and pinball. Its two well-lit rooms are filled with small game tables, chairs, and couches, just like the interior of a home. Music, TV shows, beeping and buzzing pinball games, and the murmur of a couple dozen people chatting fill the rooms. The local hairstyles and clothing look just foreign enough to suggest the early 1950s. Adults enjoy bottles of beer or ale on tap while the children purchase snacks and soft drinks, playing games with each other. It's much cheerier than American bars and not so isolated as being at home with only your own family.

The Sherborne students join in, joking with the villagers, drinking beer, and playing games. I start out trying to be sociable, drinking juice and eating some chocolate, making conversation, but it isn't long before I return to Sherborne House, seeking the quiet of my dorm. As much as I wish to feel connected, I'm also missing time I used to have alone.

It is lunchtime the next day when I run over to the Post Office, a few doors down from the Social Club. Toby, a curly-haired and rosy-cheeked Englishman, accompanies me. Once the course starts, we will be discouraged from leaving the property, we're told. Going into the village usually means one thing for me—chocolate. The Post Office is also the general store and, aside from the Social Club, the only business in town. Harry the postmaster is a balding gentleman with a fringe of dark hair and a smile for us all.

From Harry I learn that the spunky Jack Russell terrier I often cross paths with in the upstairs hall at Sherborne, is his dog. Oliver always looks so purposeful, it never occurred to me that he didn't live with us.

Harry asks us, "What kind of school *is* Sherborne?"

I'm a little surprised by his question since Sherborne operated all the previous year. The answers he's getting from Toby and me can't be of much help. We don't describe anything in the same way. Toby emphasizes some kind of cosmological system he's read about in a book by Ouspensky, some planetary arrangement having to do with hydrogens. Though I've read the book I don't understand it. Seeing that Harry's expression looks as mystified as what I imagine my own to be, I tell him about *Witness*, Mr. Bennett's autobiography.

"For me, I'm hoping the course will help us become the best we can be and that he'll teach us practical ways to continue our personal development throughout life."

I have to admit that Harry doesn't seem to show any more recognition of what I've said than he did for Toby's explanation. And, of course, the program hasn't even begun. Who knows how Mr. Bennett will be describing it?

As Toby and I return to the property we consider what different backgrounds the students come from. Some had been in Gurdjieff study groups; others from yoga, Subud, Sufi, Buddhist, or Western religious traditions; and others yet from social activism or from Mr. B's teaching of systematics, each one speaking their unique truth.

Toby says, "During our course, Harry will have the good fortune of being able to ask the same question one hundred and one more times."

"Poor Harry. Do you think he'll ever get the same answer twice?"

Later in the day, Toby and I learn from some first-year students that Harry persists in trying to understand this unusual school that doesn't fit his expectations: male and female students, some conservative looking and some flamboyant, ranging in age from their late teens to their seventies, and from so many different countries.

On another day, in the kitchen courtyard, Oliver, Harry's dog, posts himself near the woodpile, only leaving it to greet human friends passing through on their way to work in the garden.

Mick, who has just caught up with me, yells, "Quick, turn around!"

I catch sight of Oliver racing from us to the far side of the courtyard. In a split second, he catches a rat that has set foot outside the wood heap and snaps it up with a shake to break its neck. I stand there with my mouth hanging open while Mick looks pleased, as if Oliver were his own protégé.

During kitchen duty, Morgan, a swarthy Irishman, and I discover that we both own the same Cynthia Gooding album of folk songs. Singing and laughing while scrubbing the huge pots, we challenge each other to remember one song after another. Only the Work veterans' clucking disapproval alerts us to the fact that we are doing something we aren't supposed to. We sing:

The life of man is but a span
He blossoms as the flower.

He makes no stay.
He is here today
And vanished in an hour.

The next time I speak with Mick about practical work, he says, "Last year's students did a lot around here. The building had been abandoned for years. Before that, right after World War II, it had been a boys' school infamous for inspiring the 1968 film *If.* Did you ever see it?"

Not that avid of a filmgoer, nevertheless, I *had* seen it. It was about an armed rebellion in an exclusive boys' school.

Mick asks, "Remember how the film presented English society as being so authoritarian and hypocritical? Here the class system is more distinct than in America."

I picture the phantoms of those suffering young men drifting through the halls. Would we have to exorcise them from the building? Mick's voice shakes me from my reverie.

"The first year students shoveled away rubble and dust, replaced broken windows, patched holes in the walls, painted the entire inside from top to bottom, and brought in the kitchen equipment, maintenance supplies, and bedding. They also had to establish accounts with all the vendors—dairy, groceries, coal delivery, electric power, and waste service—everything an institution this size needs for daily life. And they couldn't do any of it until they were living here."

I cringe to think of how it must have been to live in such a mess. "It's hard to believe what they accomplished in ten months," I say. Yet, as busy as we are with the ordinary running of the house, I speculate about whether there are any important things left for us to do. And, if there were, where would we find the time to do them?

HAVING FUN SHOULD BE TAKEN SERIOUSLY.

Stephen Millich

Students from the first year who are staying during the transition pass on their knowledge to us, whether it has to do with animal care or how to replace windows. Bob is described as an inventor; his head of curls seems to illustrate creative ideas springing from his brain. Apparently he'd invented ways to solve mechanical difficulties in the furnace and the commercial apple peeler with missing parts. Tom watches over the greenhouse. Most of the old students seem appreciative of each other's talents and, in general, they radiate a soothing peace when we newcomers are fussing over something like whether we'll get a meal prepared on time.

Tom, a tall brown-haired Englishman with a serious face, broad forehead, and large blue eyes, is leaving soon and asks me if I would take on the greenhouse cucumbers and tomatoes he's been nurturing. The task for the cucumbers is to pinch off the male flowers, leaving only the female ones whose stems swell as they become miniature cucumbers.

The tomatoes are buggy with aphids. As he shows me how to cut away the worst branches, I ask him why certain members of the staff a so grumpy. His forehead furrows as he tells me they are emulating a teaching style that aspires to be unsentimental so that people will learn not to be distracted by superficial emotions.

"We call it 'the Gurdjieff Work face.'" To illustrate, he
turns his expression to stone with such skill that it startles me
to laughter changing any discomforts I have about excessive
solemnity into another wave of optimism about the course.

Only occasionally do the first-year students speak of the philosophy underlying their studies. Mr. Bennett, the driving force
behind the school, had studied with both G.I. Gurdjieff and
Gurdjieff's most renowned expositor, the Russian philosopher
P.D. Ouspensky. Their path of inner development is called the
Work or The Fourth Way. Although the names are often used
interchangeably, The Fourth Way is considered a manifestation
of the Work and refers back to the three traditional spiritual
paths: the fakir whose mastery is of the physical body, the monk
whose path is devotion or the heart, and the yogi whose path is
knowledge. Each method emphasizes only one aspect of human
nature and usually isolates the student from everyday life. The
Fourth Way is a spiritual path without permanent institutions
and incorporating the body, heart and mind. It is meant for
people who are fully engaged in the world—in it but not of it.

According to Mr. Bennett's autobiography, *Witness*, he
heeds his own spiritual path while remaining busy with daily life.
His profession in the coal industry had required him to travel
extensively in the near and far East. While there, exercising his
gift for languages, he had met respected spiritual teachers and
explored techniques and exercises that are still an active part
of Eastern spiritual experience. Mr. B intends to share what he
thinks is needed and appropriate for people in our culture. Sherborne is to give us a foundation of spiritual education, separate

from the dogma of a specific religion, while we remain involved in the activities of ordinary life. It seems an ideal way to learn.

As a youngster, the lack of answers to my childhood questions made me lose interest in asking. Only after becoming an adult, did I grasp that my questions were the kind that children and philosophers always ask. What is it like not to exist? I couldn't remember not being alive and couldn't imagine non-existence either. What is the meaning of life? What are we here for? Why is there so much suffering, and what can we do about it? Just formulating the questions made the adults around me anxious.

"There is no meaning."

"You shouldn't be thinking about things like that. You're just a little girl."

When they answered like that I would choke back my tears. I didn't understand I was being reprimanded for putting them on the spot. Reading *Witness* reawakened those childhood questions. Mr. Bennett believes it is imperative to ask what our purpose on earth is and intimates it has to do with becoming capable of cooperating with greater powers.

My early forays into philosophy became too frustrating to continue on my own. Answers I read or heard to the questions seemed theoretical in addition to being conflicting and obscure. I still don't know how to unravel them; Mr. Bennett, however, promises practical applications.

IF WE DON'T CHANGE DIRECTION SOON,
WE'LL END UP WHERE WE'RE GOING.

Professor Irwin Cory

4 ❧ ARRIVALS

*Unless we feel great compassion for mankind
we can't do our work in this world.*

JG Bennett

During the transition period, new students arrive daily. Everyone has a story of how they came to Sherborne House.

"I studied with Mrs. Popoff," is a statement I hear repeated several times. Mrs. Popoff, an active member of the Gurdjieff Foundation, had also been a student of the philosopher P.D. Ouspensky and worked with Gurdjieff when he came to New York City near the end of his life in the late 1940s. She runs a Gurdjieff group on Long Island and prepared a number of her students to attend Sherborne. From what they say, it sounds as if they had done a lot of Movements.

Some students come to Sherborne with their friends from other study groups or know Mr. B through his writings or his community at Coombe Springs.

Mayvor, an adventurous Swedish woman, met Mick, who had been a student of Bennett's at Coombe Springs, on a bus in India. He had suggested she come. Rumor has it that she is at Sherborne to break her drug addiction.

One student tells about her friend Linda who had been on the first course. Instead of making a spiritual quest by traveling to India like so many of our contemporaries, she had been tracing her American cultural roots back to England, hoping to meet an Englishman who understood the meaning of life.

On the flight over, she sat next to Ada, who was on her way to Sherborne. Although resistant to Ada's insistence she take Sherborne's address, Linda's fruitless search propelled her there a couple of weeks later. When Mrs. Bennett met her at the door, she acted as if they'd all been waiting for her.

One of the American students tells us he learned about Sherborne when a book of Bennett's fell on his head while he was perusing the 'esoteric' shelves in a bookstore. Another American says he was invited to attend a public lecture Mr. B gave in Boston. "I never attended lectures," he says. "For some reason I went to this one and was mesmerized by what he had to say. Mr. Bennett spoke about the hard times that were sure to catch up with us because of the imbalances within our institutions and how man was interacting with nature in a destructive way. I'd been studying ecology and reading the economist Schumacher, the social critic Theodore Roszak, and John Lilly who was researching consciousness. Coming to Sherborne just seemed like the way to bring all these ideas together." Each person's tale includes at least one unlikely event that contributes to the feeling that having found Sherborne was some kind of magic.

I tell my new friends about the dream I remembered when I'd gone to England with Mom and Aunt Mary last spring. I had awakened from the dream infused with the radiant beauty of the land. This was the kind of dream that the psychoanalyst C. G. Jung called *numinous*—expressing a spiritual magical intensity. The dramatic dark blue rolling clouds and sunlit hills as our plane passed Windsor Castle to land at Heathrow had brought it to mind. I'd had it ten years before, and when I got home I scrambled to find it in an old dream notebook:

The English landscape is brilliant. Forest and grassy hills spread before me. An orange glow to the rock outcroppings show that the sun is low in the sky. A disembodied voice is saying, "You can see why the tribe would choose a site like this." The henges are like ruins of ancient temples with columns and capitals of a leafy design I've not seen before. Nevertheless, they evoke a familiar enchantment. Then, I am standing in a shallow cave listening to a man being interviewed about why he chooses to live there. He says he often drives across the land with its rocky formations rather than take a modern road. I'm thinking such a drive is impossible. He explains that sometimes he does get stuck but the beauty and contact with the natural world is incomparable and worth the trouble. "Besides," he adds, "if one drives the modern road, there is nothing to see."

Sherborne's prospectus reflected those words.

INSIDE OF EVERYONE IS THE NATURAL, BUILT-IN DESIRE
TO BE WALKING THE RED ROAD, OR TO BE
SEEKING A RELATIONSHIP WITH THE CREATOR.

Don L. Coyhis

One of my new friends, Ivo, tells me how he's come to Sherborne. "It was unintentional. I picked up Toby, your post office companion, when he was hitchhiking on his way here. Everything he told me sounded so intriguing that I decided to hang around to find out more."

I've never heard the name Ivo before. He has the odd charm of a character in an English farce—thin with a substantial graying handlebar mustache. Maybe he doesn't actually wear khaki Bermuda shorts and a pith helmet but that's how I always envision him when not actually in his company. Anyone would guess him to be a retired military officer, so close to caricature is the look he's cultivated.

He says he's going to stay here for a little while but isn't yet convinced he'll join the course. I'm fervent about wanting him to stay because although he must be in his sixties and I'm thirty, like old buddies, we often laugh together about the idiosyncratic nature of the place, its weird mixture of warmth and gloom. But whenever we discuss his signing on, he looks into my eyes with regret.

"I just can't stand the desolate atmosphere, the unsmiling reminders of how serious our tasks are. Won't it only get worse when the course begins?"

FLOGGING WILL CONTINUE UNTIL MORALE IMPROVES.

bumper sticker

All in all, the snarling orders and gloom are countered by feeling energized from the newness of the experience, group meditation, and nourishing laughter with certain people like Ivo. I can still suspend judgment. Besides, I can't imagine leaving when, from across the ocean, the school appeared to be exactly what I'm looking for. Don't I believe Sherborne will provide understanding about the meaning of life and the purpose of human existence? And won't we learn how to bring that meaning into our daily activities?

The population continues to increase day by day as the beginning of the course draws near, and, with it, a growing tension that juggles my guts. About twelve days before the official opening, I stand in a long line of students at morning tea to collect the cup poured by April, who is on morning service. She's a tall woman with a big voice and what I think of as a charming English accent. Her straight dark hair swings forward as she bends over the teapot, a vessel so large, she needs both hands to lift it. Later, when the level of tea is a good way down, she adds more hot water to top it off. A treat of cookies, which the English call biscuits, is part of the ritual. In particular, they're fond of a whole grain biscuit called digestives which makes them sound healthier. Nevertheless, I usually pass on them because of a tendency to get the shakes from eating wheat. On occasion they serve digestives that have a chocolate coating. Those I can't resist.

The dining room where morning and afternoon tea takes place has high windows along one wall, yet dim lighting and dark wainscoting keeps the room in shadow. Oversize portraits of the Dutton family, Sherborne House's original owners, still hang on the walls. It's easy to imagine them looking over our shoulders wondering, "Who *is* this ragtag collection of people?"

I meander toward comfort in a room packed with more new arrivals—a table with a familiar face that creates a calm in me amidst the din. Lucas smiles and waves me to an empty place on one of the benches. He's a short man, at least a head shorter than I, yet his huge voice can be heard above the ruckus. In an extravagant gesture, he brushes his sandy hair away from his eyes. He's English, theatrical, larger than life, overcoming any shyness others might have about his height.

Everyone sitting at the table is male, the five of them carrying on a pensive conversation. I am sitting at one end, my attention drifting in and out of what is being said. I keep losing myself in looking at them, all a few years younger than I. In contrast to the shared cerebral discussion, by appearance they are as different from each other as the plants in the garden. It is as if the Italian film director Federico Fellini has selected them for a mob scene. Lucas introduces Ronald, the most ordinary looking one of them, neat short brown hair, brown eyes, normal weight, average height, thick black eyeglass frames.

I greet him and then turn my attention to Warren who is tall and puffy. The pasty tone of his skin, his being somewhat overweight, and the gray college sweatshirt and sweatpants all add to a lack of definition. Although young, he wears coke bottle thick glasses. Maybe he has some health issues. Both he and Ronald are American.

In a wheel chair sits Leo, whose tawny chin-length hair looks chopped as if from a self-inflicted hashing. Honey-colored skin and pale blue eyes contrast with sharp horizontal features that gravity seems to be crushing. His cunning observations cause regular outbursts of laughter, yet I can't stop looking at the distinctive sweater he's wearing. Red and tan horizontal stripes emit so much energy that it appears to be living a life of its own. Lucas surreptitiously explains to me that Leo has a terminal bone disease, which explains his unusual appearance.

My post office buddy Toby is here, too, a spare fellow not much taller than I, with circular gold wire-rimmed glasses and a mop of dark brown curls. He has that English translucent skin and rosy cheeks that make him look as if he's just come in from a brisk walk. An avid fan of the zany, he reenacts for me, at a moment's notice, skits from a popular British comedy show called Monty Python that I've never seen. The hijinks of our classmates are always reminding him of them.

As I continue to take in this little batch of new acquaintances, I feel an odd nostalgia toward them as if I were standing in the future looking back, or as if I know them from the distant past. They are so themselves, so distinct, so enchanting. Focusing on this one group sitting at this particular long table among a dozen crowded tables, each decorated with a vase of fresh-cut flowers, quiets me, keeping at a distance the buzz of excitement that only moments before had my innards vibrating.

NOSTALGIA ISN'T WHAT IT USED TO BE.

Peter de Vries

5 ❧ ANTICIPATION OR TREPIDATION

*The way to come to true sanity
is just to see things as they are.*

JG Bennett

I am assigned to do house cleaning chores with a tall husky Irish American named Patrick, who looks to be in his forties. The majority of students are in their early twenties; a few are a good deal older, and a few are in their late thirties or forties. It doesn't seem as if many are my age. Patrick, speaking in a gentle voice, looks directly at me with intelligent blue eyes.

Only when he speaks using Fourth Way Work vocabulary about the importance of being able to recognize the number world we are in and finds me unresponsive is there a lapse in his sympathetic manner. Is he offended by my lack of familiarity with the philosophical teachings? But that will be taken care of when school begins.

"Would you like to come with us to Beshara?" he asks, explaining that he, Wade, and a few students who know each other from California are going to spend two days at the nearby Sufi community. Because the course is not yet in session, we can leave our work assignments to go sightseeing as long as we let someone know that we aren't going to be around. Patrick's ex-girlfriend, Janie, is living at Beshara.

"She's a natural healer, and I've been teaching her how to combine energy work with massage therapy."

"That sounds interesting." And the fact that she was an ex was also appealing. I may have come to Sherborne for enlightenment but it wouldn't hurt to find the love of my life either. So many of the students are here with old friends, and I'm lonely for a companion.

Patrick says that Janie had been contemplating coming to Sherborne, too, but decided she preferred the gentleness of Beshara. The rigidity of Sherborne's environment plants little doubts, but I take the firmness to mean that people have a positive conviction about something they value.

I've been at Sherborne House just three weeks, yet a day at Beshara is enough to make me miss Ivo, Toby, Lucas and a few others whose easy laughter already provides me with a sense of personal friendship. At Beshara, we are guests, mostly eating and meditating. It takes time and a different effort to make the kind of conversation that feels like you're getting to know someone.

The surrounding landscape isn't so tidy as it is around Sherborne village. A wild feeling of centuries-old England produces both an inexplicable familiarity and the feeling of a different era I feel reluctant to enter. When I ask to pray in the sanctuary, I am told that as a visitor I'm not allowed. Instead, I sit alone on a hilltop overlooking unkempt brush and deserted hills watching the sun go down.

In the month before the course begins, we are introduced to only one meditative exercise. It is called the 'I AM' exercise, and we perform it during a daylong practical work session. Every hour throughout the day a bell is rung. At that moment, we stop our work and inhale "I," taking in spirit, prana, the surrounding universe, feeling one's being within the torso, then exhale "AM", feeling one's being moving outward, flowing over, becoming part of the earth, unified with all of creation. The sense of flow brings to mind the tarot image of a cup floating in a blue sky among the clouds, water pouring into it and out of it at the same time.

Sometimes the sound of the bell is intrusive, imposing its reminding presence into whatever my mind is busy chewing on, bringing me back to the exercise. At those times, I resent having to leave my thoughts. By contrast, at other times, the reminder of the bell is a balm, quieting my frenzied digging with its suggestion to breathe deeply, to see with clarity what is around me, and what I've lost contact with during my preoccupation.

AS WE WALK . . . WE'LL FIND EXPERIENCES LIKE
LITTLE SCRAPS OF PAPER IN FRONT OF US ALONG THE WAY. . . .
THEN, ONE DAY, WE WILL HAVE ENOUGH SCRAPS OF PAPERS TO . . .
READ THE INFORMATION AND TAKE IT TO HEART.

Uncle Frank Davis (quoting his mother), Pawnee

Mr. Bennett's arrival, several days before the course is to begin, raises the atmospheric clangor to new heights. He is one of those people whose entrance into a room can be felt even when you aren't looking. I catch my first glimpse of him from across the dining hall. He stands heads above everybody, about six foot five, bony, 75 years old, with a shock of white hair, bright blue eyes, and a gaze that bores through anyone caught in it. Can he read minds?

He makes me think of Carl G. Jung or Albert Schweitzer. It's that mustached upper class appearance. Wearing an aged hound's-tooth sports coat with brown leather patches at the elbows, he looks a classic model of the imposing English gentleman. Here is the person I'm putting all my hopes on. Will he bring lucidity to my search for meaning?

With him are Elizabeth, his wife who must be about thirty years younger than he, two sons a couple of years apart, the younger in his late teens, and two pre-teen daughters. The children aren't on the course but participate occasionally in various activities and, of course, live in the Bennetts' apartment when they aren't at school.

Each day the increase of crackling energy makes the air buzz and my stomach clench. I can see Mr. Bennett across the room at meals, talking with people who seem to know him. What do they talk with him about? Feeling out of place, I keep reminding myself of the numinous dream of England, how the feeling of promise had played a role in drawing me here. Am I not looking forward to communal living and shared spiritual practices? Our activities promise to reveal how ordinary daily life can be an expression of a spiritual one.

I am so animated by the energy that I often have trouble falling asleep at night. I long for a feeling of union, though it isn't clear with what. One night, tired of tossing and turning, I creep down two flights of stairs in the dark to pray in the church that can be entered from the rough stone hall near the Bennetts' apartment staircase. After sitting a short time, just as I'm about to leave, the sound of approaching footsteps in the hall make me freeze in place, holding my breath as the door gradually opens. It is Morgan, my kitchen-singing partner.

"Jeez, Morgan, you scared the hell out of me."

The church bell pealing twelve times drowns out his greeting. We decide to have our own midnight mass. Morgan prays aloud. "Please, Lord, create in us a stronger bond to the spiritual life." I'm surprised he's expressing my wish as well. His prayer segues into our singing a folksong and then waltzing to our own music. The tightness in my throat loosens tears and reminds me of a dream I'd awakened from in a sweat a couple nights before. I am leaping down the street and with each longer-than-possible leap I scream: Help! Help! Help! After I tell Morgan about it, we sit next to each other for a few mute minutes. I am praying silently, too self-conscious to speak aloud. Is he praying, too? Then, we bid each other goodnight and depart to our respective rooms.

As curious as we are about our fellow students, we're discouraged from talking during gardening or housework, and I resent being reminded not to speak. I think I know the difference between being distracted from doing my work and being able to work while talking. But my actions are often put to question by a staff person in charge of the task or by one of last year's students.

I distract myself from these thought-provoking issues by adding to the general busy-ness of the day with little projects of my own, such as sewing by hand a long skirt and a double-thick wrap from some soft flannel-like material that has a colorful modernistic print. A bookcase I construct from crates and wood scraps is so funny looking—like some squat elemental—that it makes me laugh every time I look at it. Task-free moments at tea or after meals often send me flying to the dorm, sometimes to follow through on another creative idea, and at other times, to lie down and close my eyes for a few minutes of respite. Compelled to activity from sunrise to bedtime combined with continuous companionship is suffocating. And the course has not even begun.

I am, for the first time in my life, preoccupied with prayer, an activity perhaps provoked by my disorientation. One of my classmates has placed in my hands a thin volume by Brother Lawrence, *The Practice of The Presence of God*. Brother Lawrence was a lay brother of the Carmelite order in Paris. He died at the age of eighty in 1691. The monk's simple description of turning every ordinary occupation into a reminder of God's presence suits my increasing need for solace. Why am I finding it so hard to be here?

Prayer and meditation entered my life only a couple of years before in a less consuming way. I took a vacation at an Edgar Cayce summer camp retreat for two weeks. The four fifteen-minute meditations each day lent an atmosphere of friendly support to the gathering. Meditation there revealed things I didn't necessarily like seeing about myself, such as how disparaging I felt toward people I didn't even know. But meditation showed these failings from a more generous point of view. It was as if a voice were saying at the same time, Well, you'll get over it. You're just afraid of people because you hadn't been treated very kindly yourself.

Camp fed my hunger for a compassionate spiritual life and started me on a new path. In just a few days it established a regular pattern of meditation and prayer and expanded my attitude toward everyone I met. But here at Sherborne the atmosphere doesn't feel so supportive. Instead, the snappishness of the staff and certain Bennett students brings back old feelings that create a need for vigilance.

THE WORLD IS MY LOBSTER.

Henry J. Tillman

II

THE EXOTERIC PHASE:

THAT WHICH
IS SEEN

Mid-October to Christmas Break, 1972

6 ❧ THE COURSE BEGINS

This work has service at its apex not as its foundation. At its foundation it has understanding what our situation really is.

JG Bennett

I awaken this morning, the official first day of the course, from a dream filled with a great sense of promise:

> I discover that I have a baby which Mr. and Mrs. Bennett have been caring for. After spending just a few moments with it, I feel so much love that I know I won't ever be able to leave it again.

It is Sunday, October 15, 1972, and the whole student body is gathering together in the ballroom for Mr. Bennett's opening address. My one hundred and two classmates drift in, each finding a place to sit. Mr. B sits on a chair wearing that same hound's tooth jacket that seems to be his uniform. Most of us are sitting on cushions scattered on the floor before him. The air is dense with expectation and quiet chatting. Everyone has arrived, even the latecomers. While we wonder why Mr. B is not beginning, impatience is added to expectation. Finally, we realize he's waiting for us to silence ourselves. At last, when we become fully attentive, he speaks slowly, welcoming us to Sherborne and asking us to remember why we've come here. Then, with great deliberation, he describes the culture most of us live in, and the historical epochs of human evolution.

He says, "These significant periods are speeding up and moving more quickly than ever before. The most recent one of the last several hundred years is based on the belief in the sacredness of the individual. However, the imbalances of energy created by our gigantic institutions require the development of a different kind of consciousness built on support and not on power over each other. Institutions are not flexible enough to respond to the coming challenges. We need to understand the purpose of man's existence and what his role might be in the cosmic scheme of things. We are here at Sherborne to learn what it is we humans do not know about ourselves that keeps us from living a peaceful, sustainable, and continuing existence."

He speaks about the ability of man to create energy, his weaknesses regarding greed and hunger for supremacy, and his inability to put spiritual knowledge into practice. He refers to higher powers that require us to pay a debt for our existence, that we have the ability to create our souls, and that we are not automatically born with them. I don't know what to make of this.

His British accent lends convincing authority to the American ear. Each of his long pauses underscores his weighing every thought before he says it aloud. We're not used to the intermittent silences which make many of us squirm.

I need to hear these reminders of why we are here because for the past month the daily schedule and grim company of some Work veterans have disheartened me despite moments of pleasure. He speaks to us for well over an hour. During the discourse, his meaning seems clear but, as soon as he finishes, little sense of it remains. Only two concepts about the school stay with me.

First, he warns us that we cannot be free until we are free of our petty likes and dislikes—toward people, things, activities. "You will have many opportunities here to learn more about yourselves by opening to new experiences. You can learn much by choosing to do what is unappealing, attending to the people who don't attract you, performing tasks you think you cannot do; in other words, by putting aside your usual inclinations. Ultimately, we must be capable of living the way that we believe is just and loving."

I recognize that by having agreed to be at Sherborne House, I am going to experience life in ways I might not agree to under ordinary circumstances. The protected environment allows us freedom to conduct ourselves in a way that is different from our usual responses. There are no grades or prizes, no certificates of completion, no competition created by outer motivation, no punishments or penalties. Theoretically, this should free me to try activities that I do not know how to do and to experiment with my behavior toward people as well.

Will I be able to make this year more meaningful than my past schooling where I didn't like the way we studied history by memorizing dates and simplistic reasons for the cause of war instead of studying real documents and human behavior? And what about jobs where I spent hours filing papers or pasting in word corrections on supply catalogs? Then I think about former colleagues who gossiped and took pleasure in causing dissension. I wonder if I'll have the courage to make choices based on my values instead of my preferences.

The second concept that Mr. B introduces addresses some of my questions. He asks that, in every situation and with every exercise, we verify as far as possible whether our new activities serve the purposes and understanding we have determined for ourselves. What is our personal aim? This simple notion is to become our touchstone for evaluating everything, including the Work as we are being shown it. He also implies that by acting from our own conscience we will connect to a force beyond our comprehension.

YOU CANNOT GET WHAT YOU'VE NEVER HAD UNLESS YOU'RE
WILLING TO DO WHAT YOU'VE NEVER DONE.

Mac Anderson

So, once again, a sense of promise counters my discomfort with Sherborne's atmosphere, and we begin the official program of physical labor and inner exercises. This is how the daily activities are organized: The student body of one hundred and three people is divided into three groups of about thirty-five people each. Every day, one group is on house duty—cooking, cleaning, and childcare—while the other two groups attend classes in cosmology, psychology, movements, and lectures on other topics that aren't necessarily ongoing. In the mornings, however, everyone works in the garden or on property maintenance for two-and-a-half hours. Only those whose housekeeping tasks have to be performed during that time are excused. Lest we become too comfortable with our accomplices, we are forewarned that the groups will be reconstituted several times during the ten-month course. Since every student plays every role, by the end of the course we should experience all sides of every practical activity.

Warren, of the gray sweat suit and coke bottle glasses, is my group's house supervisor the first Sunday of the course. It was his duty to allocate jobs on the Saturday night before. The house tasks include sweeping the infinite hallway floors, chief cook, assistant cooks, potboys, childcare workers, assorted maintenance projects, and washing and pressing sheets. Even though the full list of assignments doesn't necessarily go up on the board that night, at least the supervisor must notify the morning servers and breakfast cooks. They have to put the huge pot of porridge on the coal-burning Aga, a cast iron stove, to cook through the night, and the morning servers set the tables after dinner is cleared. If they learn of this duty very late in the evening, they have to return to the dark dining hall where the dim lights feel eerie, and the sound of utensils echo as they're being set upon the tables in the deserted room.

We are told we may go to church on Sunday as long as we let the house supervisor know so he can assign us afternoon and evening chores. Although I'm Jewish, I decide to go, thinking I am already in need of another break since the one I took by going to Beshara was a couple of weeks ago. Going to church will provide a formal outlet for my spiritual yearnings, I decide.

When I informed Warren on Saturday night that I intended to go, he said okay. However, in the morning the list shows me assigned as lunch cook for which I need to work through most of the morning. I seek him out.

I ask, "Don't you remember that I told you I was going to church? I need the morning to cook." Is he purposely sabotaging my plans? Of course, I don't say that to him. He is unmoved by my reminder—unwilling to make any changes, and I feel stuck.

I remind myself of *The Practice of the Presence of God* and decide to follow Brother Lawrence's simplicity of intention. Cooking the soup will be my Sunday prayers. I hold this thought in my mind as I cut and sauté the onions and carrots. In addition, I make it a point to pray hourly. So immersed am I that I'm barely aware of the other cooks in the kitchen or what they are doing. The efforts *do* change my angry state and the soup turns out okay. Later in the day I apologize to Warren for what I think of as lashing out at him.

Not long after this incident, I notice that I'm still carrying negativity toward Warren. I've already seen at close quarters the variety of ways other people solve similar problems. Instead of agreeing not to go to church when he'd scheduled me to work, I could have told him without any anger that he had made a mistake, that I had informed him the night before, and he'd agreed to my going to church, which I still intended to do. Then I could have gone off on my journey and let him deal with finding someone to take my place. Stating my position and doing what I thought fair without his agreement would never have occurred to me at that time.

As I imagine myself behaving differently, however, additional aspects to this incident become conspicuous. There was my need to get approval, for one, and so after presenting my case logically, and still not getting permission, I did as I was told while inwardly nurturing defeat and resentment.

In the case of my wanting to go to church, the purpose was to give myself a break when *I* felt like having one. Had guilt over this unstated purpose contributed to my lack of resolve about going? I want to think that giving myself a break is 'taking care of myself,' not just selfishly doing what I feel like.

Maybe I was afraid of Warren, whom I didn't even know, being angry with me. Or was I even more afraid he would report my shirking to Mr. Bennett? What if *he* disapproved? He could kick me out of the program. Or what if Warren didn't assign another cook to take my place, and I became the reason there was no soup for lunch at all? Then *everyone* might become furious with me. All of these thoughts and more are what Mr. Bennett calls 'inner considering.'

CONSCIENCE IS A MOTHER-IN-LAW WHOSE VISIT NEVER ENDS.

H.L. Mencken

Mr. B keeps after us for grumbling. Students must be saying things to him or to the staff about how cold it is in the house, what our diet is lacking, or the ways in which our fellow students aren't up to par.

"You're too quick to look for comfort," he says, "never learning what you're capable of accomplishing. Don't forget to work with your likes and dislikes. Stretch yourselves. See what new attitudes you can cultivate."

I keep thinking back to high school and college in Chicago —the cold and wind, the schedules, the way we were expected to feed back the teachers' exact words. I'd hated it, feeling that nothing I worked for was worth the effort. I earned my degrees, and got good grades keeping in mind only one goal—to get out of school. Almost all my academic goals had come from other people. The closest I came to inner direction, once I was done with school, was a continuous string of hybrid aims, combining a direction I wanted to go in with something that might meet parental approval. Now I try to understand Mr. Bennett's idea that back home I'd had all the elements needed for a rich spiritual life. Just how can I make this experience different?

On class days, work in the garden begins at 8:30 a.m. I wander out to the courtyard where all the students gather in silence to await gardening instructions. The sun is almost a white disk hanging in the gray southeastern sky—a comforting, though pale presence—before it burns off the heavy morning fog.

Gardening never ceases. We weed, dig potatoes, harvest spinach, and turn soil in preparation for spring. Everyone wears layers of clothing to fight the damp chill. Gum boots known as Wellingtons or, "Wellies," are needed for clumping around in the mud. Only a quarter of our class needed to purchase them, as most of the first year's students left theirs behind. As the morning wears on, discarded sweaters and scarves appear to be growing in the garden like intergalactic flowers opening to the warming air.

We are each given specific tasks and if seen doing something different, we're reminded, "Don't forget to struggle against your preferences." Then begins the inner considering: Is what I'm doing a mere preference or a response to what I perceive to be a need of the garden?

A CONSCIENCE IS WHAT HURTS
WHEN ALL YOUR OTHER PARTS FEEL SO GOOD.

Steven Wright

Pierre, our Movements teacher, also directs much of the gardening. I frequently see him racing down the garden path as fast as he can, often pushing a wheelbarrow. He appears to have made a pact with himself to race everywhere he goes. I don't think I've ever seen him walking. Today, without the barrow, he is bounding in ballet-like leaps past the spinach toward the doorway that leads to a second garden and the green house. He trips on something and hurdles to the ground. But before I can run over, I see him rise up like a marionette on strings, dust himself off, and leap away at breakneck speed, following his original trajectory.

We are taught to care for the garden tools, including our Wellies, by rinsing the mud off at the end of the period. The ice-cold water used to wash the hoes, forks, and spades before storing them away in the shed at the end of each work session leaves our hands stiff and red.

Toiling in the garden is softened at first by moments of quiet conversation, though as we become more used to working in silence and discussing only what is needed regarding our tasks, talking to comfort ourselves becomes less needed.

On our way to morning tea, Toby and I come upon the lupines. "Lupines!" he calls out as if seeing an old friend. Then he launches into telling me about another of his favorite *Monty Python* TV skits. A robber based on Robin Hood steals lupine bouquets from the rich and gives them to the poor. The robber's destitute recipients are sick of being given stolen bouquets. They rail at the robber.

"We've eaten roasted lupines, cooked lupine soup, and sautéed them in oil. We've made lupine sorbet and worn the bloody things. Can't you please bring us something more practical—like gold or food?" The robber, meanwhile, is scribbling on a notepad as fast as he can, as if he cannot otherwise remember what it is that people really want.

The most ordinary tasks often take on unplanned outer complexity because of the ongoing edict to observe ourselves. It is not unusual to come upon people in the garden or in the house moving slowly like zombies, their eyes unfocused and their limbs not swinging, as they put all their attention on trying to sense their bodies while walking to the next task. My reaction to seeing them alternates between laughing as if I'm watching one of Toby's *Monty Python* skits and being reminded that this is an exercise I should be trying out myself.

On my way to the housework assignment one morning, I meet Nancy, a shorthaired older woman, in the hall. She tells me she still needs Wellies. Although she wears my size, I observe myself not offering her mine because I feel lazy about going up to my third floor dorm to get them. After we part ways, I keep thinking about whether I should get past my reluctance to go upstairs. I am on my way to meet Toby who is assigned to kitchen duty. Our plan is for me to take his place in the kitchen for the short time he needs to do me the favor of rewiring my lamp.

When I arrive at the kitchen, it turns out that Nancy is there, talking with Mary, the white-haired matriarch of kitchen supplies. Nancy is explaining that she needs to find some boots before being able to pick spinach in the mud. Seeing this as a chance to redeem myself, I pipe up. "I'll get you mine."

Before anyone can say a word, I run out of the kitchen racing all the way up to my third floor room at the other end of the building. By the time I return breathless, Mary is handing Nancy some boots she's found for her in the discarded clothing room.

I protest. Mary dismisses my complaint kindly by saying that I had good intentions, but I don't let it go. I am annoyed, feeling as if my run, which I'd been reluctant to make in the first place, now turned out to be for nothing.

"Why did you do that? You knew I was going all the way up to my room," I complain.

Now Mary is annoyed. "You butted into Nancy's and my conversation. Besides, if you didn't have a personal interest in getting Toby, who should be working in the kitchen, to do something for you, then you wouldn't have gotten involved in our business. You're suffering because your motives weren't pure."

That stops me in my tracks. I already felt conflicted about whether to help Nancy. Then I thought I was overcoming my laziness. Now Mary has added a new element. What does Toby doing something for me have to do with Nancy? Well . . . it is true we aren't supposed to be doing each other's jobs. Toby and I *are* manipulating the system even if it is for only fifteen minutes. Also, even if Nancy used my boots, she would still need to have her own which she is now acquiring permanently from the used clothing room.

But I can't help pointing out to myself that Mary is telling me I've butted into her conversation when, in fact, Nancy and I had been talking about this subject before Mary got involved! I hate being criticized and I hate seeing how much I want Mary to approve of the effort I've made. Surely I am being misunderstood. And what about this motive thing? Is every activity going to bring up some hopeless conflict? Will I always need a lawyer to sort out what is fair or unjust?

THE FIRST PRINCIPLE IS THAT YOU MUST NOT FOOL YOURSELF—AND YOU ARE THE EASIEST PERSON TO FOOL.

Richard Feynman

7 ❧ HOW THE SCHOOL WORKS

Bearing things is work on oneself.

JG Bennett

At the opening of the course, Mr. B had requested that we give up any other spiritual practices we might be doing, such as yoga or particular meditations. "In the ten months we have together," he had said, "I will be teaching you specific techniques and exercises. It is important that we share the same experiences so that we can develop a shared language for speaking about them. This shortcut will help us develop common ground in the limited amount of time we have."

I had wondered why he didn't keep it more like real life, where we come from dissimilar backgrounds and have different practices and then must learn to communicate with each other about our experiences despite the differences. Now I see he also believes the shortcut is necessary due to lack of time.

The only two conditions for admission to Sherborne are a genuine wish to learn how to live more effectively on all levels and a readiness to work hard to find the answers. I try to embrace the challenges Mr. Bennett sets before us. Ten months isn't very long for giving his ideas a chance to prove themselves.

Nevertheless, giving up practices that I've worked so hard to acquire contributes to my feeling adrift. With great effort, I'd turned around years of profound depression and physical illness to achieve greater stability than I'd ever had. Still, I can see that without my familiar diet, chiropractic, meditations, and psychotherapy, it might be possible to experience the affects of new techniques.

Without intending to be rebellious, I see that my mental habit of resistance, developed from trying to navigate the demands at home and school, is embedded to depths beyond my control. Every assignment at Sherborne draws the same kind of inner struggle I felt back then. So much of my youth was spent working hard to meet expectations and living on schedules that never reflected my internal rhythms. Not until I was a few years out of college, had I even begun discovering pulses that rise from within, including my choosing to go to Sherborne. Now, here I am with Sherborne feeling and looking a lot like my school of old. I have some serious sorting out to do.

HABITS ARE FIRST COBWEBS, THEN CABLES.

Spanish Proverb

Whenever Mr. Bennett discusses a subject with us, he reminds us to speak from our current encounters and observations, not from ideas about the subject. If a student talks about working in the garden with another student, she may be asked a number of questions. Is it relevant to the story. Who were you with? Which garden? What were you doing? What tools were you using? What did he say? What was your reaction? The attention to details makes it clear we are talking about a real situation and not generalities or an interpretation of thoughts about a subject. It demands thinking differently and brings a refreshing reality into most observations.

Yet there is also specialized Fourth Way vocabulary, phrases such as 'remembering ourselves,' 'intentional suffering,' and 'being identified' that become rote in their usage. People with Work experience often use them to shame instead of for teaching the concept. Those who recognize how jargon can be used mechanically make fun of the Work veterans by calling them Bennetrons.

Barry, a member of our service team today, says, "Hey, I've got an idea for how we can save hot water when the wash and rinse waters get dirty." Three of us are in the room with him. We stop washing dishes for a second to listen to him.

"Instead of changing the water in both sinks when the wash water is dirty, let's put soap in the rinse water and use it for washing. Then we only need to replace water in the wash sink and use it for rinsing." Another serviceperson, long time in the Work, snaps, "Oh, Barry, you're too identified," perhaps meaning that Barry's attention is directed outward and that he has none left for inner awareness. Barry's suggestion is simply dismissed as if it weren't worthy of attention. I think that if Barry does have something to learn about identification, it isn't going to happen through this type of dialogue.

The exchange makes me wish I could introduce a Gestalt psychological exercise called *active listening*, but there is always a negative reaction whenever a reference to psychology is made, unless Mr. B is speaking. In the *active listening* that I experienced, the person who is the listener reflects the ideas expressed by the speaker by putting them into his own words. This simple exercise always reveals how the listener's feelings color the way he is hearing what is being said. The task is complete when the speaker can say to the listener, Now I think you hear what I mean.

For example, a husband might reflect his wife's stated wish to travel someplace exotic for a vacation by saying, You always think it's stupid for me to go fishing, and she might say, You never want to go anywhere I suggest. If they don't get caught up in their reactions, they might instead make plans together for an exotic trip to Fiji that includes deep sea fishing. But there is never time to explore ideas from other traditions. It is not what we are here for.

Regarding news from the outer world, Mr. B suggests, "Don't listen to the radio or seek TV and newspapers. And if you make a habit of filling your time by reading, don't do that either. Give yourselves the opportunity to live in a different world."

The schedule is so full that we have little time for those things anyway. And who has a radio or television? I get all the news I need from Vinnie, a quirky New York music journalist. How else would I have learned that a man who called himself, Dan Cooper skyjacked a plane and demanded $200,000 in cash and four parachutes with a claim he had a bomb in his briefcase. Cooper jumped with the money to be never seen or heard of again. I enjoyed hearing news from Vinnie's rock-and-roll point of view, a claim I would never make about conventional news programming. But where does he get his information? Does he go to the social club every night for TV?

> TELEVISION - A MEDIUM. SO CALLED BECAUSE
> IT IS NEITHER RARE NOR WELL-DONE.
>
> *Ernie Kovacs*

Mr. B does not allow us to take notes during class. "Often, you cannot take in what you are hearing when you are preoccupied with writing," he explains. "Extend yourself. Listen with care. If you wish to make notes later in the day, after class, then do so. See what you remember and what makes sense to you." His comment allows me to continue keeping a journal. In fact, before the course began, I had purchased a new book to write in, optimistically putting a quote on the first page. "There are no problems to a soul—only opportunities for growth."

I wrote down a quick exercise Mr. B had us try regarding attention. In describing it, he reminded us about sensation, that is, directing attention to a place in the body so that one feels it from the inside. In this case, we were to combine sensation with feeling from that same place in the center of the chest where "I" exists. By closing our eyes and saying, "I see" from that place of combined sensation and "I," when we opened them and looked, we saw differently. He said the same could be done with hearing or the other senses.

More often than not, when I write in my journal, it is in an abbreviated way, such as, "Ivo and I laughed about the cold and the sad message that seemed to underlie Mr. B's lecture." But if I look at it even a couple of weeks later, all I have are questions. What about the cold did we laugh at? What sad message in Mr. B's lecture? Lecture about what? Those cryptic notes to myself don't work out very well, since I never take the time while memory is fresh to fill in the details.

Theoretically I can do it because within three months of beginning the ten-month course, the half-hour at morning and afternoon tea, an hour for breakfast and lunch and an hour-and-a-half at dinner begins to feel like generous quantities of time, allowing for any private business, exercises we are to do in our spare time, or relaxation.

One soothing ritual develops following lunch during the frosty weather. Perhaps a different half-dozen students each day, wearing layers of work clothes and down vests sit on the pavement outside the south wall of the building. The concrete walk and two jutting walls of the house only a few feet deep and about twelve feet apart soak up the sun and reflect its delicious heat on us. Crouching against the wall, we sit with our knees up, lazing in what we call 'the sun pit.' Sometimes there are discussions, but just as likely we all sit with closed eyes.

Someone might murmur, "Ah, . . . the hot generosity of the blessed sun."

"Mmmmmmmm," the rest of us answer.

Each day begins at 6:00 a.m. when one of the two breakfast cooks rings a bell to awaken us, striding through the halls like a town crier. At 6:15 the bell is rung a second time. We have been instructed by Mr. Bennett to perform morning ablutions that are based on Islamic ritual. With cold water, before our ordinary wash-up, we rinse ourselves: face, eyes, ears, and mouth, drawing water in and blowing it out from the nose, waving a wet hand across the top of the head, wiping water from elbow to finger tips, rinsing our private parts, and wetting the legs from knees to toes. Icy as I get, I find it warming.

I always awaken with the first bell. Finding it too torturous to lie there knowing I'll soon have to get up, I prefer to pop out of bed, throw on the red candlewick robe over my ski pajamas, slide into fuzzy slippers, and get to the tubs before anyone else. As usual, all three tubs in the ladies' bath near our dorm are grimy from those who bathed late last night. With great annoyance, I wash out one of the filthy tubs because after ablutions I look forward to bathing in a couple of inches of warm water and watching the steam rise in the frigid air. I also rinse out the tub when I'm done. *I* am a good girl.

Never do I ever wash the tub, before and after my abbreviated bath without sending a flood of invectives to whoever left it dirty. Never do I find the tub clean or ever think about using the situation to strengthen my inner patience. It must just be too early in the morning to take this sacred opportunity for personal growth. Today is one of those rare moments when I happen to notice what I'm doing. I console myself by remembering Gurdjieff's story of the village bell ringer who knew how to benefit from the energy of daily curses sent to him by those who did not like being awakened. Maybe the tub spoilers are more conscious than I am and can benefit from my tirade.

Being on the move at that hour, I can bear bathing in the icy tub room, but no number of layers is enough to keep me warm during the forty-five minute meditative Morning Exercise that follows. I wear long johns covered by the plush-like floor length skirt I'd sewn before the course began, hiking socks, tee shirt, turtleneck, jacket, mittens, and a fluffy orange poncho that looks as if I am wearing my bedroom blanket over it all. Yet I still can't keep my mind from the cold. The meditative concept of watching one's breath is a literal act, it often being colder in the stone building than it is out in the daylight.

IT DOESN'T MAKE A DIFFERENCE WHAT TEMPERATURE A ROOM IS,
IT'S ALWAYS ROOM TEMPERATURE.

Steven Wright

Morning Exercise begins at 6:45 when we file into the grand ballroom, leaving our shoes outside the door—a perfect set-up for occasional children's pranks. Their best trick so far is when, with what I imagine as joyous glee, they knot together dozens of unmatched pairs, forcing harried teamwork to free them while breakfast is still available.

The huge rectangular space of the ballroom dwarfs the grand piano that stands in front of the short wall of windows at the far end. The tall windows along the long wall and the short wall let in plenty of light except in the middle of winter when the sun doesn't rise until we are almost done. The ceiling must be sixteen to twenty feet high with swags of baroque plasterwork on a couple of walls that never cease their bizarre contrast with the bold abstract paintings covering the long wall without windows.

Mr. Bennett sits on the floor with his back to the piano at the far end. The women sit to his left facing the long wall of windows and the men sit to his right facing the women. Just inside the entry on the women's side are stacks of cushions and a few kneeling benches that can be taken to place. Some chairs and benches are already set up on both sides for the older folks.

Mr. B introduces a new meditative Morning Exercise each Monday. He directs our attention to one point after another in our bodies, beginning at the center of the forehead, moving down the left arm and leg, then up the right side. He says, "Attention is a material substance. During the course, we will learn how to create and direct it. We must be able to direct our attention. It is essential for doing any Work in this world." Again he reminds us of sensing, which requires directing attention to a specific place in the body and feeling it from inside.

Sitting on a cushion on the floor is so uncomfortable, I'm positive that I won't be able to remain seated that way and attend to the exercise. Somehow, I manage to muddle through. Whichever way I choose to sit each day—whether cross-legged, on my heels, or using a kneeling bench—I've gotten the message that it is imperative for practice to sit in that way throughout the entire Morning Exercise. It's probable I put more attention on sitting than on the meditative exercise. I am trying to do it right. Others are making the same efforts. It isn't all that rare for someone to stand up after Morning Exercise and faint from the change in their blood pressure or fall flat on his face with his first step because his legs have fallen asleep. That obvious dedication becomes an unspoken mark of honor.

Each week's Morning Exercise becomes more complex, demanding greater attention by adding five breaths, relaxation, or increased sensation to each point. New variations are built on the foundation of previous weeks' practice. Mr. Bennett always introduces the new Morning Exercise by talking us through the steps, once or maybe twice, and then in silence we repeat the meditation on our own until the end of the period. When forty-five minutes have passed, we stand up to bow three times. Mr. B calls this eastern tradition "the rukus" (pronounced roo'koos).

During the rukus one morning, I see myself in temple at Rosh Hashanah. I'm ten years old attending the service with my friends. Few of our parents attend even the adult services. After prayers in Hebrew that I don't understand and translations that feel unrelated to our lives, the rabbi tells us to pray about the Korean War. I'm glad to be directed to do something useful. My mind fills with the images we see on the TV news every night. Why are we sitting in our warm houses watching men kill each other? I am searching for the right words to wish the soldiers safety and to beg the universe to help humans make peace, but the rabbi's angry voice intrudes. He is saying the prayers for us, and he sounds like war. His words cut my connection to something that was trying to form. Give me a few minutes, my inner voice begs.

Now it is Mr. Bennett's voice that is calling me back. In my paradoxical relationship to ritual, while hungry for its meaning, I am repulsed by demands to perform it exactly as it has been done in the past with no accounting for the present circumstances. But this is different.

The first bow, he explains, is to the higher self, the second to that which we share with others, with all of life, and the third to that which is Divine or unfathomable. Time expands as I bend from the waist with my hands on my knees holding these thoughts with whatever words I choose to express them. Mr. B's reminders to do the rukus create a sacred stillness in which to express gratitude for each of those elements of life and to feel the relationships among all that is.

LIVE AT THE EMPTY HEART OF PARADOX.
I'LL DANCE WITH YOU THERE, CHEEK TO CHEEK.

Rumi, translated by Coleman Barks

8 ∾ OUR DAILY LIFE

You can actually be much closer to a person when you can bear their manifestations than if you're upset by them.

JG Bennett

I am still getting to know the students in my group and becoming more familiar with the classes and exercises that are an essential part of the course. Patrick, the burly fellow who invited me to Beshara before the course began, is in my group. After lunch today we start talking about back pain. I tell him how my back is still sore long after dragging my dumpster-sized suitcase across Reading station. "Years ago I'd been told that the only option left was surgery, and even so they couldn't guarantee a cure. Instead, I followed a friend's advice and started seeing a chiropractor. It keeps me functioning without drugs."

"A good massage will relieve pain better than a chiropractic adjustment," Patrick says,

I'm not sure I believe him but he offers to massage my back
in his room. I'm not ready for any hanky-panky though I am
attracted to him. I'm hoping he's right because, as grateful as I
am for learning about chiropractic treatment, I've never come
to terms with the jarring force and bone-crunching sounds of
having my spine adjusted.

Not knowing Patrick that well, I break out in a sweat as we
walk down the corridor. He has one of the few private rooms.
Anyone could have asked for one. It just costs more. He opens
the door and enters while I follow cautiously. The space is neat
and clean and the intimate size of a room in an ordinary house.
He invites me to lie face down on his twin bed. In addition to
having a gentle touch, he seems to know what he's doing. I can't
remember the last time I had such tender physical contact, and I
soak it up like a sponge. He methodically moves his hands up my
back, each stroke moving out from the spine, beginning at the
pelvis and working his way up to my shoulders. When he discov-
ers sore spots, he kneads them away with just a little pressure.

This is so different from getting an adjustment—gentle
and pleasurable. Best of all, I learn that it works. The discomfort that had been plaguing me for weeks is gone. After Patrick
is done, he lies down next to me, and we embrace. Tentative
kisses lead to longer ones, yet we close our eyes and almost fall
asleep. Something returns us to alertness, and we go off to our
afternoon class.

When Patrick and I talk more about our studies, he con-
trasts the instruction from Bennett with living at Beshara.

"Beshara is a peaceful atmosphere separated from the outside world and filled with love. Here, at Sherborne, we deal with that outer world and learn to keep the peace within."

Does he really think of Sherborne as being part of the outer world?

Patrick continues, "It's important for me to work in the manifest world and not avoid it or stand separate from it—like the Jesuits."

Does he mean the Jesuits stood apart as priests or is he comparing the Jesuits' call to action in the world as being like Sherborne? I never get around to formulating the question.

Sometimes Patrick and I are assigned the same house duty and so we begin to know each other better. I like that he is artistic, taking well-composed photographs of the beautiful land around Sherborne House and of our activities. He encourages me to use my camera, too, but I am too self-conscious to take more than occasional pictures within the classes or while we are working.

Today is the first time I'm assigned to the morning service team. It means we've set all the tables the previous night, and this morning cut the loaves of bread into fourteen slices each, for toast. We also put out marmalade and a dark brown tar-like substance called Marmite on each table. Marmite is a salty/savoury aged yeast ex ıct that the English eat with the same enthusiasm Americans have for peanut butter. After breakfast we'll clean up, return food and cookware to the kitchen downstairs via the dumbwaiter, sweep the dining hall, and wash the dishes and eating utensils in the servery next to the dining room.

At breakfast, unlike the other meals where diners are served, everyone queues up and walks through the servery, picking up a slice of toast from the cooks and a bowl of porridge from Mr. Bennett, who uses this opportunity to look us over. The chief cook asks me to tell the four people on a.m. service with me what our task is during breakfast. "We're supposed to serve coffee and tea to people while they're eating," I tell the others.

Boris, a tall lanky German with a handlebar mustache, serves coffee for a few minutes and then sits down to eat. "Hey, we're not finished serving," I tell him.

He glares at me. "I haff done my share—one-fifth—and dat is all I am goink to do." Had he counted the number of people at breakfast and divided them by the number of servers?

Out of a misguided need to make up for Boris, I feel compelled to keep serving hot drinks throughout the whole meal, never taking time to eat until the room empties. I join the other servers in the servery to wash dishes. Patrick, who is one of us, comes into the room after I do. He is scowling and refusing to talk. Now what? After dealing with Boris, I am unable to bear any more crossness directed at me. At least with Boris I understand where he is coming from even if it is stupid. Patrick's fuming has me flummoxed. All I can think to do is pray for enough understanding to get past this latest sensitive moment. Was this how it was going to be all year, nothing but strain and misunderstanding with people whose ideals I thought I shared?

Half an hour later, Patrick comes over to me smiling, all the tension a thing of the past. He reaches down, enveloping me in a tender one-armed embrace. I slip my arm around his waist in a timid gesture of greeting. This seeming-apology from him still gives me no clue about what his problem was but I'm satisfied knowing that through some mysterious process his anger has vanished.

Patrick and I spend more time together, but whenever I am with him I feel as if I am being assessed and found wanting. My disinterest in the Work vocabulary tests his patience. Steady references by Mr. B to our not making enough effort and our inability to be awake, let alone transform, are dispiriting. I spent my life making efforts for parents and teachers who were never satisfied. If I earned a B+, I would be asked why hadn't I gotten an A?

Does Patrick take my apathy for Work language personally? I guess if he values the language and I reject it, he might feel like it was a rejection of him. He is as reactive to my disinterest in his Work loyalty as I am of his critical way of relating to me. You'd think our shared sensitivies would help us gain some insight. There are times when I ask for an explanation of what he is angry about. He speaks of triads from systematics and centers of our functional being, language I can't even replicate. I may not understand the meaning of his words but I understand the feeling I'm left with. Maybe that's why he doesn't speak in plain English.

INVARIABLY ESCHEW THE UTILIZATION OF
AN AGGRANDIZED WORD WHEN
A DIMINUTIVE ONE SUFFICES.

Anonymous

Adding to the emotional confusion is the friendly affection Patrick and I share. When we aren't talking about the Work, I admire his soft-spoken observations about the challenges of life at Sherborne, and I enjoy his gentle physicality without the intense intimacy of making love.

Mr. Bennett mentions how when a person is being unpleasant, some people say to just ignore him; don't pay any attention. But then he mystifies me by adding, "It is a great mistake not to face the unpleasantness, as it provides a very fine substance almost impossible to get in any other way."

Hearing about this special energy generated by conflict encourages me to apply the philosophical lesson to my blossoming love life. Maybe Patrick and I can continue cultivating our relationship by transforming those moments of annoyance or hurt into something positive. Aren't we being given tools? Attention. Breath. Sensation. Who knows what the possibilities are?

And I wonder, what does Mr. Bennett do with *our* energies when so many expectations and opinions are directed at *him*?

The sacred dances called Movements are scheduled more often than any other class—one to three times a day. They come from spiritual traditions in the Middle East, and were taught by Gurdjieff to his students in the West. After his death, Movements continued to be passed down through Gurdjieff groups that were still active in Europe, North America, and South America. Some of these groups practiced the same Movements for years. Yet it is when you don't know them that they demand the kind of attention that changes one's inner harmony.

Each of our teachers knows slightly different versions, often taught to them by the same teacher, and much discussion centers on trying to identify which are the 'correct' ones. Aren't they mistaking form for essence? Thomas de Hartman, with Gurdjieff's guidance back in the 1940s, had written music to accompany them. Several Sherborne students who play piano are groomed to play for our classes. The music is rhythmic and compelling, just as I find the Movements themselves to be.

Although Mick and Anna also are Movements teachers, Pierre teaches us most often, his wife, Vivien, usually accompanying him. They are at Sherborne with their three children, the oldest of whom is on the course. Mick, who had lived at Mr. Bennett's community Coombe Springs, most often directs work in the kitchen; but he also guides garden activities and teaches Movements. Anna, we are told, had met Mr. Gurdjieff in Chicago when she was only a child. Her hair, pulled back in a tight bun, is dyed black and is in stark contrast to her white skin and bright red lipstick. She reminds me of an Edward Gorey illustration, a mysterious and moody Victorian character gliding about in a long dress and fringed shawl, haunting us throughout the year.

When Pierre speaks, my ears prick up, having to listen with greater care to understand his odd French/British accent. Purported to be Mr. Bennett's nephew, Pierre looks alert with his high forehead, black hair, and fringe-like beard with no mustache. For Movements classes, he wears a regular shirt and pants with cuffs tucked into bulky red socks, his outfit completed by white ballet slippers with elastic across the arch. It is known he had been active in the French Resistance during World War II.

The idea of such a dangerous and secret role increases the image of shrewdness he cultivates and which we all affirm. Between Movements and gardening, we see quite a lot of him.

The students dance with bare feet since socks are too slippery on the wooden floor. We dress in ordinary lightweight clothing knowing we'll soon get warmed up despite it being cool enough to see our breaths. I often have icy bluish hands and feet while working up a good sweat.

Throughout my childhood I had taken several kinds of dance classes and found Movements to be different from all of them. The ninety-degree angular arm and hand gestures remind one of ancient wall paintings and contrast with the graceful smooth motions of ballet and the natural motions of most folk dances.

Movements feel primordial, often conveying a state of being rather than emotion. Pierre greatly enhances their effect by the way in which he teaches them. He does not point out when mistakes are made. Instead, stopping the music, he repeats his explanation or again demonstrates what we are to do, then asks the pianist to begin again. This 'no blame' model places the burden of effort on each of us to discover whether we play a role in causing the need for repetition.

Movements are introduced to us in parts. First, there may be the pattern of the head, turning it to the right, then to the left, up and down; then the arms without the head movement; then the feet; then, perhaps, movement of the files in which we stand. The parts sometimes have different counts so after learning them separately it is more challenging to put them together. Conflicting counts make it impossible to use the brain to do the organizing. It forces the body to figure it out by doing it. For some students, working from the body comes naturally. Maybe they are innate athletes. I find it both frustrating and exhilarating. It commands a pleasant physical exertion that I haven't experienced since the hard play of childhood.

During Movements class, we also do exercises that Pierre creates in the moment, such as walking in place to a piano rhythm. We might be stepping according to a 1-2-3 count while counting with our voices 1-2-3-4-5. Another task is to copy changing foot rhythms while holding our arms out to the side, parallel to the ground. All of us have different reactions depending on the mood of the moment. Sometimes I feel infuriated over having to work so hard or lighthearted with exuberance toward the challenge. One day, just as I become certain that my arms are going to fall off, all of a sudden they begin floating in the air beside me. I've gone through some kind of wall I might never have experienced unless I took up running marathons. From that time on, I can expect breakthroughs to happen.

At the end of a Movements class, it is suggested that we sit for a few minutes and say an invocation silently. "May the results of my work enter within me" or "May the energy raised by my work be transubstantiated within me," or whatever words we want to use to honor our efforts and the help we are given. The invocation can also be coordinated with directing attention to our limbs, one after another, in pattern.

Teachers at Sherborne often make reference to our having three centers: intellectual, emotional, and physical or moving center, each of these having higher and lower expressions. At other times we are told that each center also has intellectual, emotional and physical aspects to it. Movements and our other activities help us see how we might be using only one or two centers rather than a balanced measure of all three. With practice, it becomes easier to see how this is the case and why it might be useful to experiment with equalizing them.

Pierre is teaching a very complex movement. He does not explain the Movement to us in the usual part-by-part manner I've come to expect. This time, he just performs it with all its contradictory rhythms expecting us to pick it up by imitation. He's stopped us half a dozen times within a few minutes. Without the distraction of personal confrontation, I'm able to attend to challenging myself. Still, I just can't do the Movement.

Pierre never says a word while I, on the other hand, am merciless to myself. Come on! Get on with it. Pay attention! You've only ever done what was easy for you. No wonder you never learned how to do things that were difficult. You never learned *real* persistence. What's wrong with you? I sound like the meanest schoolteacher ever. I even make myself cry just as sure as if some impatient coach were yelling at me.

At the same time, I continue my fruitless attempts to do the Movement while my mind is blathering on about my experience when I was in elementary school, how we wasted so much time on rote tasks and competition. And how there were way too many kids in the classes—forty-eight. If we made a mistake we were never protected from being mocked by the other students. It was easy for me to get good grades but I never had to stick with something I couldn't do well right away.

Meanwhile, my persistent attempts to do the Movement continue failing. Something makes me aware of all the energy I'm expending on anger, resentments from the long distant past, and tears. An unintended moment of reason intrudes. Could I use the energy wasted on bullying myself instead to learn how to do the Movement? I'm still weeping with frustration, yet manage to stop berating myself. At the same time I'm also considering and resisting a profound urge to run out of the room. I don't know what keeps me from leaving—a glimmer that this experience could shatter old habits that prevent other possibilities—I'm learning how to learn. Maybe it's Grace that makes me keep trying. I don't know how long it takes, but the reward finally comes. I'm doing the complex configuration. More than the satisfaction of doing the Movement, however, is the wonderment of having stayed in the room, for what feels like the first time in my life making it past tearful exasperation. I know at that moment I'll never speak to myself the same way again. And I know now I have a choice of how to behave, when in the past there didn't seem to be any.

At the end of class, as usual, we sit in our places—silent—absorbing the energy of our efforts. On this occasion we sit for a very long time, and I have an uncanny sense that Pierre is praying for us. . . .

9 ❧ INTRODUCTION TO THEMES

Everyone has an inner teacher,
But we have not yet learned to go to that school.

JG Bennett

From the moment I arrived at Sherborne House, I've felt unable to meet the expectations. The quantity of silence only increases an unpleasant self-awareness. How can I assess what I'm experiencing? Time and again, I'm repulsed by the snappish tone of voice used by staff and old Bennett students. While I use the same tone when feeling critical of them, I search among my classmates for tenderness to smooth the rough edges. At the same time, the systematic way of looking at the world is similar to the sparse and analytical communication I was brought up with. Although it is unpleasant, often missing important expressive cues, it is familiar and I believe what I'm being told—that it signifies discernment. It is also clear to me that no matter how hard I work at something, *I* am always dissatisfied with the outcome. Since we are told every day to ask more of ourselves, I don't know where or how to reasonably draw the line.

It is November, and Mr. B keeps our after-dinner Movements class long after the usual 10:00 p.m. ending. I am brimming with indignation about this breach in the schedule that makes the day's activities last even longer than usual.

All *I* can think about is how I've already put in my time today. I don't need another forty-five minutes of Movements. Let me go to the dorm and tune out. I sound a lot like Boris when he was serving breakfast. I remind myself that I chose to come to Sherborne and that I have nothing else to do with my time tonight.

After class, other students are raving about how lucky we were to have had Mr. Bennett teaching the class himself and extra time for Movements! I wonder at the intensity of my habitual resistance in contrast to their excited embrace.

Two weeks before Thanksgiving, Mr. Bennett says to us, "In your spare time after all the classes are done for the day, see if you can finish up the work on the stable block building in time for the Thanksgiving holiday." I overhear students making plans to meet at the stable block at 10 p.m. after Movements. In my mind, I ridicule the enthusiasts, as if all of them are foolish to believe that the deadline means anything. I'm so overwhelmed by the full schedule, the meditative exercises, the constant stream of new Movements to learn, and Mr. B's philosophy that I need to keep pushing everything away.

I remember observing a crawling baby watching some toddlers running back and forth. You could see her strong wish to run. Her eyes followed the children as they scurried back and forth, and she laughed when they laughed. It reminded me of having an interest in life that seems to have disappeared. Many of the other students are so enthusiastic about everything, I wonder if there isn't something wrong with me. Have I lost a natural satisfaction that comes from trying new activities?

Second-guessing my intentions and rationalizing them to others and myself is getting tiresome, again, driving me to prayer. And who am I praying to? I know what I am praying for, usually just to get through another day, to carry out the commitment I made to myself to stay the course. I've pretty much forgotten about any lofty aspirations.

> FANATICISM CONSISTS IN REDOUBLING YOUR EFFORT
> WHEN YOU HAVE FORGOTTEN YOUR AIM.
>
> *George Santayana*

On Monday mornings, Mr. Bennett introduces a way of studying called a Theme. It provides a matrix for self-observation. He explains how we are to approach the assignment.

"In Western culture we often make a mistake in thinking that if we read about something or have seen pictures of it in a magazine or a show about it on television, we now understand it. Therefore, we are to take great care in speaking not from thoughts and concepts about the topic but only from our direct experience with it."

Mr. Bennett speaks about our responsibility to the material world and the power we have over the tools we use. He asks us to notice how we relate to them, encouraging us to set ourselves tasks that could deepen our understanding. For example, if we choose to deprive ourselves the use of something that we often employ, such as a pencil or shoes, the consequences of not using them will increase our awareness of their role in our lives. He reminds us that we are not talking about our thoughts on the Theme, but incidents or experiments.

"Observation combined with experience is what will create understanding," is how he puts it. He also cautions us, "Don't disperse your energy by sharing your experiences before the Theme meeting on Friday when we will discuss them. Let the pressure build."

I have no ideas for tasks or experiments. I just try to digest what Mr. B suggests as an approach to the Theme—to observe real events. His ideas about working with a topic of observation are similar to therapy when I wanted to change some of my attitudes about events that I called hopeless. I've noticed that if I don't talk with friends about what I am trying to do, I seem to make more successful efforts.

It is Friday, and we're meeting to discuss the Theme. I've done nothing to actively experiment and so all I can do in preparation is scan the week in my head to see if I noticed anything. I'm surprised to discover I spend more time and energy relating to tools than to people.

From the minute I awaken in my down blanketed bed wearing warm pajamas, hearing the bell, putting on a robe, using a wash cloth, towel, and tub, not a moment throughout the day is spent without using tools, relating to them, or interacting with other people about them. How big a pot do I need for the spinach? Where is the other push broom? It should have been obvious to me how embedded we are in the material world.

During the week, there were some free-floating images, possibly relevant to the Theme because tools were involved. However, they stick in my mind like dreams, making little sense. One day I came across two hand spades for gardening, each left in inappropriate places—one in the elegant stone Great Hall on the ground floor and the other in the stable block, the old stone building we are to renovate by Thanksgiving. Maybe there, someone thought the hand spade would work as a passable pointing tool to replace old mortar. When I noticed them, a question arose about responsibility: Was I going to put them away where they belonged or just leave them where they'd been abandoned? After finding the second one, I decided to go back to the first and put both of them away.

The second free-floating incident happened a couple of days later. I was walking along the front of Sherborne House enjoying the well-designed view of the hills with their intentional groupings of trees. I passed Byron who was walking in the opposite direction. I noticed that I was carrying some wire wound into a circle about eight inches in diameter, and he was carrying a hammer. The image persists in my mind. I carry it into the Theme meeting, yet I have no memory of what either of us was doing with those items or what kind of observation I can make about them.

I also recall watching several students leaving our ornate home carrying pick axes over their shoulders. They're not usually stored inside the mansion or are they? Nor could I imagine at that early hour that they'd been in use somewhere inside. All I could think of was how strange everyone appeared holding tools that didn't make sense in the surroundings.

Friday Theme observation takes place in the downstairs library. Mr. Bennett sits silently, waiting until everyone brings their attention into the room. This is how every meeting and lecture begins, making us aware of our habitual tardiness or inattention expressed by mindless chatter. Eventually the atmosphere becomes hushed and somber. I am alert to the images floating around in my brain, but no words are sitting on my tongue.

> IT'S SO SIMPLE TO BE WISE. JUST THINK OF SOMETHING
> STUPID TO SAY AND THEN DON'T SAY IT.
>
> *Sam Levenson*

As the tension grows, it becomes ever more difficult to break the silence. Who will dare to speak first? When someone finally makes an observation, a long pause hangs in the air before Mr. B makes a comment. All I can think of is my wish to hide. What if he doesn't wait and instead calls on me? I keep willing myself to become invisible. Maybe that's the unconscious reason for writing to mom and asking her to mail me my camouflage sweatshirt. "I can really use it here," I told her.

While I panic, others participate and the Theme observations are unexpected and diverse, inviting Mr. Bennett to elaborate on them. He often finds something of great value that I wouldn't have recognized. One man describes treating tools poorly, short-changing his care for them. "All I seem to do is take and never give back." After a short silence he adds, "I guess I don't have any real experiences to report."

"When did you discover this attitude about taking and never giving back?" Mr. B asks.

"This week."

"In fact, you have made a very great discovery. I hope that you will be able to retain this realization. If you can do so, it will be the beginning of an immense change in your life."

Another student tells us of his proprietary attitudes; another of how ubiquitous tools are in life, and he wonders if this requires some duty on his part. The omnipresence of tools had been so central to my experience that it hadn't seemed to be an observation. Mr. B comments that we've become very dependent on tools.

"But there's no going back to a primitive life without them. We must come to see that this relationship demands that there is a price to pay. We must see whether we waste material resources, how they are shared, and how they affect the environment. Do they pollute it? What is our relationship to them? Can we allow tools to be all they can be without interfering with another aspect of life? Just a small amount of growing awareness allows us to become normal about developing respect for them. Because we have so little to do with the production of the tools we use, it has become normal not to respect them and not to understand the far reaching consequences of their use."

I can't help but think of bulldozers and chemicals used for processing plastics, packaging waste, and other industrial activities.

Sometimes, Mr. B is harsh in his comment to a student, calling him to task for laziness, but a minute later he is sympathetic toward someone else or expansive to such a degree that it inspires awe. Does he know who benefits from a blunt awakening and who requires a gentle touch? Still, I can't imagine feeling comfortable enough to be a willing contributor to the Theme meeting.

The wide ranging reactions and observations about tools help me see more about humanity's attitudes toward taking, controlling, and using objects, both man-made and natural.

When all who want to speak are done, Mr. Bennett addresses the importance of finding a right relationship to the material world. Finally he completes his talk with a suggestion of asking us to compare the right treatment and potential of a tool with right human action. "How can we use ourselves as tools, developing an awareness of our actions in relation to a greater purpose?"

10 ∾ ABOUT SILENCE

Speech is one of the harmful activities of man that prevent his spiritual progress.

JG Bennett

There is still more to our daily schedule—much of it orchestrated by Mr. B. Between his looking each student over as he serves porridge at breakfast, dining with him at every meal, his leading Morning Exercise, reading aloud to us each evening, and his introducing and closing weekly Themes, he is a constant presence. Despite classes and practical work with other teachers and his short excursions elsewhere, he seems always to be with us.

At lunch and dinner we eat in silence and begin those meals with a prayer that Mr. B wrote:

All life is one and everything that lives is holy.

Plants, animals and man, all must eat to live and nourish one another.

We bless the lives that have died to give us our food.

Let us eat consciously, resolving by our work to pay the debt of our existence.

Only for limited periods of time have I practiced prayer before a meal. I am glad to have a cue for attending to our food, even though the reminder of having a debt to pay for our existence awakens a sense of alarm. Eating in silence, however, softens the sensory overload.

At breakfast, which isn't silent, the children eat with us before going off to school or day care at Sherborne. They eat lunch and dinner earlier than the adults—under the watchful eyes of whoever is assigned to childcare.

Early in the course, the noise at breakfast tended to escalate until Mr. B would point it out. We don't have a traffic light that flashes red and sets off an alarm such as in my local school lunchroom, but as we adjust to Sherborne's unique culture, the need to talk becomes less urgent.

When first eating without talking, everyone was a bit self-conscious, avoiding eye contact. The need to signal for salt or pepper, water, or a second helping had to break through the self-imposed isolation. Now, it's almost a game to anticipate other people's needs and surprise one another by passing a platter or saltshaker before being beckoned to do so.

Without the sounds of our voices at silent meals, we learn that clamor can be caused in many ways. Dishes clatter if they are set down with a heavy hand, spoons and forks clank against the plate when we are lifting food off of it, water burbles as it is being poured into glasses. Everything echoes in the uncarpeted and uncurtained hall. In the servery next to the dining hall, servers, forgetting how sound travels, dump the dishes into sudsy dishwater and swirl the stainless utensils, attempting to loosen clinging food. When the clatter carries into the dining room, Mr. Bennett corrects the situation by making a cameo appearance in the servery. We continue to discover other ways we disturb the silence.

A lengthy crescendo of noise is filling what had been the silent dining room. Dozens of voices are speaking in a rising cacophony. I realize they are voices in my own head, and I put a halt to the internal chatter. Suddenly the room returns to an eerie silence.

IF WE ARE TO KNOW PEACE,
WE MUST LOOK WITHIN OURSELVES.

Don L. Coyhis

In addition to gaining information about stillness, we are also learning about the sharing of food. In the servery, the cook is doling out generous portions of potatoes to each plate the servers hold ready. However, he runs out long before all have been served and almost a third of us are deprived of receiving any. It can't be undone. People who have already been served their meal have dug in and are eating. The cook is distraught; the possibility of running out hadn't even crossed his mind.

For weeks afterward, all the first helpings become meager, cooks playing it safe. They offer second helpings when they

become sure there's enough. We all improve at estimating portions. Another safety factor we invent is to serve some courses
family style. It is easier to divide a course of food into ten large
bowls in the servery before the servers place them on the dining tables. Then it becomes the burden of the diners to split the
table's allotment fairly.

I'm sitting at a fully populated lunch table when I notice
someone with an angry pout pointing to the empty bread platter. Every slice is gone. I never eat any, and there are only nine
of us at the table. Three other people respond by shooting looks
of poison at one poor fellow. He's already eaten more than his
share, and despite the silence we all know who the culprit is.

We are asked to limit our speaking with each other to topics
relevant to the activity in which we are engaged. This caution
has the dual effect of making us more attentive to the tasks at
hand and more aware of what we are saying. Mean-spirited talk
while washing dishes takes on greater significance than when
such behavior is considered 'normal' as it was in our lives before
coming to Sherborne. That small amount of clarity also gives
insight into personal motivations for talking, which often are
neither kind nor logical.

Having been given some guidelines about speech, some
people feel the need to enforce silence as a 'rule' toward all conversation, even when dealing with children. What a tiresome
human trait—to take every caution and turn it into law.

Issues regarding talking resurface at regular intervals
throughout the course. When we go to the Social Club, for
example, the local residents inevitably ask us questions about

the school. The challenge is to understand what the questioner actually wants to know. When one patron of the pub remarks on the wide age range of Sherborne students and wants to know whether the school is a place for people with disabilities, he most likely does not need to hear a lecture on Systematics. A married couple that knows Mr. Bennett from church inquires about the amount of time the school devotes to spiritual practices. They are dumbfounded by being given the impression of an apparent code of secrecy relating to the daily schedule.

We each have our own interpretation of Mr. Bennett's recommendation to use discretion when answering questions about Sherborne. Nothing is secret. The question is: How should we share information in a way that makes sense to people who are not participating? Anyone can be invited to attend open weekends that comprise all the activities of the school. Can we discern who will welcome such an invitation?

The first time we spend a full day in silence, we do the sixty-point attention exercise. Every fifteen minutes when a bell is rung, we sense a different point on the body following the pattern we've been taught in Morning Exercise. The physical task is weeding the immense lawn, an undertaking akin to counting grains of sand on the beach. Yet it awes me to see how much can be accom lished in a rather short amount of time when one hundred people are working together.

On another silent workday, we are cleaning out debris from the property that is beyond the scope of our day-to-day chores. We have a huge bonfire for items that can be burned. Rubble that isn't burnable is collected and taken to the dump.

My eyes never stop watering from the smoke. The silence, focus, and length of time we work makes it feel like a personal cleansing. I experience no irritation or impatience as I often do when we work extra hard. In fact, the overall quality of the day is like looking through a veil into another plane of reality.

A couple of weeks later, Mr. Bennett asks me about my sense of that day, I tell him what I just described.

"Did you see the Virgin Mary?" he asks.

"Uhh . . . no."

Without any hesitation, he goes on to discuss other things. Later in the day, when I tell some friends about Mr. B's question, I learn that a couple of people had reported seeing Mary. I didn't ask about the visions, more concerned about whether I was supposed to have had one.

At regular intervals everyone at the school participates in a day of silence combined with a special physical task and inner exercise. Paula, a woman who could have given orders to Zeus, finds not talking so unbearable that she is awarded special dispensation not to participate. Instead, she focuses on taking care of the children, a common task for her since she has a young son. I find silent days, like silent meals, a welcome comfort that simplifies life.

Between 6 p.m. and dinner at 7, Mr. Bennett sits in a leather-upholstered chair in the downstairs library, wearing his hound's tooth sport coat, and reads aloud to us from *Beelzebub's Tales To His Grandson* by G.I.Gurdjieff. It's alternate title, *An Objectively Impartial Criticism of the Life of Man,* describes a little better what the series of three books is about. Still it doesn't convey the convoluted language, creatively re-named concepts, and humor that force the reader to consider the absurdity of human behavior including our erroneous notions about education and the possibility of purposeful human development.

This last is, for me, perhaps the one concept that keeps me feeling that Sherborne is where I need to be, despite my reaction to the dour mood of the place. Nowhere else in my experiences does anyone express the possibility for continuous human development, only improvements to the material world.

For me, even the passive activity of listening to the book being read is a formidable test. My sleepiness in the late afternoon is profound. Since my college days, it has been my habit to nap in the early evening, waking for dinner and then staying up late to finish homework or personal projects. The problem of adjusting to a new schedule is compounded by my inability to relax at bedtime.

During Mr. B's reading, I sit on the library floor along with most everyone else, prop myself against a wall or one of the few overstuffed leather arm chairs reserved for the older folks, put my knees up, and wrap myself in a warm shawl.

Compared to the rest of the building, the downstairs library feels relatively sumptuous. It has dark wooden built-in shelves, a well-worn oriental carpet on the floor, and fitted interior shutters, crafted with such expertise that they keep the cold at bay. Close to one hundred warm bodies huddle together in a singular sense of comfort. It isn't long before my eyes drift shut and sleep overtakes me. This is my pattern.

There are times when Mr. B reprimands students for inattentiveness or for directing too much care toward their knitting, one of the few automatic activities allowed during reading hour.

Never, much to my occasional wonderment, am I told not to sleep. Maybe he thinks I will learn more in my sleep than when my mind is awake to build barriers of analysis.

My exhaustion during the reading is in sharp contrast with other times of the day when our focused endeavors are energizing. I am able to do more physical work with greater ease than ever before. However, companionship with a hundred people day and night, is simply too stimulating. Time spent by myself is as necessary as food and air, so after everyone is asleep at bedtime, I bask in the quiet. The physical silence feels healing, and so does the lack of other people's mental and emotional turmoil. I might read a few paragraphs, jot some notes in my journal or, just as often, lie in the dark with my eyes open, taking in the delectable serenity.

In another activity of silence, meditation, a feeling of gratefulness comes over me for my growing ability to direct attention. How long I remain thankful, I don't know; but without noticing it, I slip into a lively internal dialogue. I am challenging a relative of mine whose remarks about my poor memory still sting. She is a teacher of learning disabled children. 'Where is your compassion for *me*?' I demand to know. And then I realize how my appreciative thoughts have seamlessly shifted to another topic and deteriorated into reproach. Now that this idea has bubbled up, I can hope that maybe, one day, meditation will also release the feeling of injury caused years ago by a thoughtless comment.

11 ❧ LIKE SHEEP IN THE FIELD

*Try to learn to come to everything as if it were quite
new, and as if it had no connection with what you
have heard before.*

JG Bennett

In lectures and classes, much attention is given to the philosophical significance of the qualities of energies, will tasks, seven lines of work, the nine-pointed figure called an enneagram used as a tool for understanding the process of transformation, and other diagrams illustrating all of these concepts. It is a fact that most of Mr. Bennett's writings are of this sort. He is a scientist and presents his philosophy methodically, requiring all of us to stretch our thinking—in my case, well beyond my natural inclinations.

It's not that I don't believe examining guiding principles to be significant. I value the world created at Sherborne where understanding human existence is considered a necessity; yet, sometimes the intellectuality feels devoid of common sense. Can't we see by the results when someone behaves poorly in the garden without diagramming the forces involved? It seems as if Mr. B and his previous students can't process information about feelings directly and need the narrowly defined authority of systematics in order to understand what occurs. For them, diagrams of triads with arrows indicating the active, receptive, and reconciling forces make it clear.

On the other hand, in the words of one friend, there are times when Mr. B speaks from his unwavering confidence in the spiritual world, and the roof opens up. Light from heaven shines down upon us. The building itself floats a foot off the ground, and we are transported to another dimension where the laws of the universe are known and seen to be beautiful. Afterward, neither she nor I can remember what he actually said.

Mr. B gives us a new Theme. He suggests that we examine what happens within ourselves when we experience 'contact.'

"Part of contact is a matter of being objective, rather than subjective," he says. "One can put one's attention into something and not be in contact with it. Contact makes one semi-objective. If you are sensitive enough you'll be able to see how an object can fulfill its function and how awareness of it changes your state, bringing you into the same world with it.

During that week, I notice a situation that seems exemplary. I am speaking with a little girl in her mother's presence. After our first few exchanges, the adult begins speaking for her child, intending perhaps to improve the dialogue, and soon the child is hiding behind her mother instead of interacting with me, as she had been when we began. As with the previous Theme meetings, the thought of bringing my remark forward intimidates me. When none of the observations are about contact between people, only with material objects, I assume I've misunderstood the Theme. I say nothing. Better to presuppose than chance humiliation.

In many of our group meetings, not just Theme, Mr. Bennett asks us a question about our attitudes or behaviors, quick to tell us he does not want to hear our answers aloud. Instead, he has

us sit in silence to think. If the question is why we did something, it is revealing to listen to my internal answer. If I spoke,
I no doubt would have given it a spin with the intent to please
someone or defend myself. His question and the privacy provide a safe place where I can tell myself the truth.

This exercise allows me to uncover and accept many unsus-
pected motivations. External honesty grows as we become more
able to admit to our real motivations, some of which, we learn,
can be satisfied in more appropriate ways. For example, a student needing attention rather than information can get a better
quality from developing friendships rather than by becoming a
demanding student. Knowing what we are really seeking makes
it easier to fulfill the aim. When lessons like this come from Mr.
B himself, they have none of the rancor that often accompanies
judgments from students.

LYING INCREASES THE CREATIVE FACULTIES, EXPANDS THE EGO,
AND LESSENS THE FRICTIONS OF SOCIAL CONTACTS.

Clare Booth Luce

My retired army officer friend Ivo is assigned the job of house
supervisor. The benefit of his new position is that he appoints
duties to Patrick and me that allow us to be together all day.

"If I could have," Ivo tells me, "I would have assigned
myself to working with you, too."

I'm so pleased to hear that our affection is mutual. I don't
know anyone else his age who feels like a colleague. The bad
part is that he is ill.

"I'm sure it's from feeling so much pressure all the time," he says, "the schedule, the Themes, the atmosphere, and now being in charge of the house. I just can't keep doing it. It's time for me to leave."

I hate hearing him say it, though I shouldn't be surprised. He warned me before the course started that he wasn't sure about staying on. Last night he dreamed about abandoning a garden he'd grown. His description makes me wonder if he's running away from some part of himself that has grown by being here. Or maybe he abandoned something important to be at Sherborne. We don't try to interpret it. I just hope his leaving isn't as much his loss as it is mine.

Tonight is Ivo's going-away party. I cannot imagine attending a noisy gathering after class at 10:00 p.m. I go to bed instead. Silence. No people. Escape. As fond of Ivo as I am, that's all I can think of.

Ivo is leaving today. I go to his room and we embrace, his handle bar mustache brushing my cheek. We exchange a long look with tearing eyes while I tell him he's been one of my most dependable sources of fun.

"What will it be like without you?" I ask. For a moment I imagine the relief I'd feel if I could leave too, yet I'm determined to fulfill my commitment to the course. I apologize for having slept through his party last night, sorry to be in overwhelmed-mode but he knows the feeling only too well. That's why he's leaving.

"Come on," he says, trying to guide me out the door. "I've got to finish packing. I don't know how I'm going to organize my books and all this stuff I've collected."

He is quite agitated. Had he come here with all these suit-cases? He seems to have worn only one outfit. I can't imagine how he ever fit the bags into his little car in the first place, and in addition, picked up Toby as a hitchhiker when they both came to Sherborne. What *are* all these books and papers and knick-knacks? I want to make up for my absence from his party, so I insist on helping him pack. Rather quickly, we get everything tucked into boxes and bags to his noticeable relief.

"I'll pack the car myself," he insists, so we make our fare-wells right there.

Later in the morning, when my activities take me past the front door, I peek out at the driveway thinking of him. Aware of a wistful emptiness in my chest, I guess I'm hoping to find him still sitting there, debating whether he should leave or not, but the driveway is empty. No abandoned pile of boxes and suit-cases either. He must have squeezed them all in. I take a deep breath of the outside air before turning my back to the door and returning to my duties.

Not many days after Ivo's departure, a violent storm causes the temperature to drop below freezing. For a couple of days practical work is comprised of cutting up a huge ash tree that was blown over, requiring sawing, splitting, and stacking of the wood. The smooth gray bark is covered along one side with green moss. All of us working look like an illustration from a fairy tale: a bunch of elves compared to the tree, our breaths vis-ibly hovering about our heads. We are dressed in bright sweat-ers and down vests, scarves, gloves or mittens, and ski caps, our colors rivaling a box of Crayolas. We use every type of ax and saw—even those six-foot long, two-man saws I'd only ever seen in photos depicting the cutting of redwoods.

As we stack the wood, I notice we're bending a sapling that can't be over three feet tall. I straighten the little tree and move the stacks to either side of it. However, when I return, I find it broken. I point out to whoever is near that "it *had* been a living tree." As soon as I hear the tone of my voice, I'm sorry to have spoken. It's a tone I so dislike when I'm on the receiving end. Besides, the damage is already done and had no doubt been an accident. If anything, I hadn't done enough to prevent its being damaged. Sandra, the one who broke it, is standing right beside me.

"I thought it was a crooked branch sticking out from one of the stacked pieces," she tells me. "I feel like I'm wrecking the pile every time I put something down on it." She was already feeling incompetent before I had my say. I've changed the merry picture of elves into this.

"I'm sorry. I should have pointed the tree out before anything happened to it. It isn't your fault."

It's hard to reconcile my snappishness with my exquisite sensitivity. Why can't I just stop behaving in ways I don't like? There are ways other than raging for getting a point across, yet I snap as often as I complain about the crabbiness of others. If I had put my attention on the sensation in my foot before I spoke, maybe I could have bought myself time until another sensibility awakened, like the old wisdom of counting to ten before you speak.

HONEST CRITICISM IS HARD TO TAKE, PARTICULARLY FROM A
RELATIVE, A FRIEND, AN ACQUAINTANCE, OR A STRANGER.

Franklin P. Jones

At Sherborne we tend to an unusual breed of sheep called Jacob sheep that belong to Anya and Keld, a couple who had taken last year's course. Each sheep has white and brown wool that has already inspired the creation of several beautiful sweaters. Some are white and brown; others have a third tone made by carding the two together. The sheep roam in the flat park-like field out front that has a few scattered trees and is where the donkeys and horse spend most of their time, too. Our task is to get the sheep into the shed for a veterinary exam.

"Here, Wooly, Wooly, Wooly!" Pierre calls. They walk right over to him, interested in the hay he holds up to their noses. Five of us students circle at a distance, holding our arms out to bar the spaces between us. Again and again we are able to herd the five sheep together and move them in a particular direction, but whenever we think we are about to drive them into the shed, one of them gets spooked and leads the rest in a breaking run through our circle.

An hour passes before we succeed in positioning them just right. At that moment, one of the donkeys saunters over to the shed entrance and stands there blocking it. We give a collective moan and begin the process once again. Our ranks swell to maybe twelve and, at last, we're able to coax the donkey away and convince the sheep to enter. It's taken two hours!

It feels as if I've just been in a Movements class—the exhilarating cold, standing perfectly still, holding my arms out forever, needing to be alert enough to block a sudden escape, then seizing the right moment to goad the sheep in.

The picture continues to play in my mind for hours—as if it's really an image of us students at Sherborne. Hungry for the spiritual food gained from our conversations with Mr. B about the meaning of human existence and wrestling with the practices we're learning yet questioning the need at times to be herded into a dark little shed.

12   ∾   DECISION

We cannot get rid of impulses in us, but we can say yes or no to them.

JG Bennett

Mr. B is about to introduce us to the Decision Exercise. We gather in the bright and airy ballroom, excitement bubbling through the air as it always does whenever Mr. Bennett is announcing something new. If we hadn't already learned a little restraint, people would be asking questions before he even spoke. Instead we quiet ourselves so as not to delay his talk by making him wait for us to simmer down. As always, he sits with his eyes closed for some minutes. I have the feeling he's assessing our state.

When he finally speaks he reminds us of the importance of learning how to carry out our intentions. "The Decision Exercise is a valuable tool that provides step-by-step experience in understanding and strengthening Will." He describes it this way:

"The first step, planning, is done at night, the day before carrying out your chosen task. Consider your reason for doing it. Ask yourself what order it brings.

"The second step is done while you are still sitting after Morning Exercise in the ballroom and before you stand up to do the rukus. First visualize and then sense in your body doing the Decision.

"Third, ask yourself, 'Am I going to do it?' If the answer is affirmative, move ahead according to plan. If you get a 'no', let the task go.

"The last step is done at the end of the day, before planning the next day's Exercise. Look at how today's Decision went. Compare it to your intention. See what was the same or how it differed. If you failed to carry it out, then you must remind the body to carry out tasks you have given yourself. Remind it with a difficult physical task such as holding your arms out for ten minutes."

The tension in the room is a mixture of anxiety over the possibility of not getting it right and excitement about learning another new practice.

"For now, keep your choices simple," says Mr. B. "Stick to the physical realm. In this way you will be able to recognize easily whether you've accomplished it or not. Don't work on something subtle or complex such as changing an attitude. Instead, learn how to sew on a button or write a letter you've been putting off, but don't do tasks you know you would have done anyway. The point is to develop your resolve. Each time you do the Exercise, it should stretch the Will and teach us something about how it differs from willfulness or self-will."

Mr. B adds something more to help us consider the Decision Exercise in relation to Will. "We do not make Decisions. We find them or they are revealed to us. There's a sense of their presenting themselves rather than their being only of our own choosing; a sense of inevitability about their being done, that they come from a deep internal connection rather than our unilateral choice."

And finally, he explains, "The Decision Exercise is to be done in your free time—during the half-hour tea breaks in the morning and afternoon, after eating meals, or after the last activities of the day. I expect you to do it every day for the rest of the course."

Every day. After chuckling about 'every day' and 'free time,' my next reaction to hearing this pronouncement is, for once, not that of being overwhelmed. The intent to carry out decisions is something I already feel a need for in life and invest energy in.

As soon as Mr. Bennett is done speaking, a forest of hands appears. The questions range from useful to having him repeat everything he's just told us.

"Can we do things that are part of practical work?"

"What if someone beats us to doing what we decided to do?"

"How will we know the answer to the question of whether it will be done?"

"What if I forget to do it?"

"Can I use it to improve my diet?"

"Can sensing my hands be a Decision?"

Questions and patient answers last for at least fifteen minutes until it becomes clear he won't be taking any more.

"At this point," he says, "it is up to you to accrue some experience and let that guide your future questions."

Though we have been told to look at everything freshly as if it has no connection with the past, I cannot help but reconsider my long history of working with decisions. My interest arises from childhood disappointments. Our parents found it hard to follow through on their intentions, and I could see it was as big a source of frustration for them as it was for my brother and I. Because of their habits, I found that I had little practical support. There was no one to talk with who could help me choose or learn how to do the things I wanted to do. This lack of guidance fed my abundant fears. As I struggled to carry out decisions when I was a teen, I received satisfaction from an assortment of unrelated accomplishments—teaching myself to crochet, sew, play the recorder, and swim. Each choice had no goal other than doing something that looked interesting or countered a fear.

Now, with the promise of practical methods for bringing actions with higher ideals into the world, being able to carry out an intention can mean something more important—helping people who are discriminated against, changing laws, getting food to starving people, how to be kind even if you don't necessarily feel that way. Life had already shown me how human efforts often fail when, despite good intentions, people don't do what they say they're going to, or personality conflicts destroy an organization. Every day the news shows examples of disagreements sabotaging perfectly good projects. Don't humans already have the scientific and psychological knowledge to improve life on the planet? Yet we don't seem to understand what interferes with practical application of the knowledge.

Although I hated school, I worked hard and got good grades, which means I had plenty of practice in accomplishing tasks that other people thought were necessary. However, when I've tried to carry out my own projects, finding ones that hold my interest enough to complete has been painfully difficult.

Now, at Sherborne, we will have the opportunity to choose tasks we set for ourselves and have the peripheral support of knowing that all of us here are trying to do the same thing. We'll share the Decision Exercise while individualizing the actual work. This is one project I embrace without my usual reticence.

Years before Sherborne, I'd taken a couple of workshops on decision-making and even practiced an exercise of my own until I left Chicago. In the one I did, visualization was used to establish how the task would be done. One of the steps that was new to me in Mr. B's version is the use of sensation to enlist cooperation of the body. It adds an extra impetus for completing the chosen endeavor.

I have Decided to re-pot a friend's prayer plant that I've been caring for. Its variegated green leaves have gotten so bushy it looks as if the pot is about to burst. She's given me a grayish purple planter to use. Once I sense in my body the act of extracting the plant from its old container and adding earth into a bigger one, I feel almost driven to completing the task. Every time I have a moment of quiet throughout the morning, the plant comes to mind. There is no rest until the job is done. It's as if my body has been activated by the sensation.

In another example, I'm preparing a Decision for cleaning up a little bookshelf in my room. Although I've done the visualizing step and see myself straightening out the books, it isn't until I actually sense the task that I become aware of trash, bottle caps and string, I've left on the shelf and need to throw away if I'm really cleaning up.

A second aspect of Mr. B's assignment that lends a different energy to the process is the step where we ask ourselves if we are going to do it. One morning when I'm still sitting in the ballroom after morning meditation and before the rukus, I ask myself if I'm going to sweep out the broom closet, the one patch of floor that often is overlooked. Instead of receiving a 'yes' or a 'no,' I receive what I interpret as a 'yes, if . . . .' An image comes into my mind's eye showing me that the broom is not going to be in the closet as it usually is. I will need extra time to search for it. When time to do the Decision arrives, the broom is not in the closet and instead of being annoyed, I am already prepared to look for it elsewhere.

Another example of 'yes, if' happens when the idea comes to me that there will be an unforeseen demand made on me during morning tea when I plan to carry out the Decision. Since I'm still sitting in the ballroom, I change my plan. I prepare to do the task at a different time of day and, having made the suggested adjustment, a 'yes' now confirms the Decision. During breakfast the person in charge of laundry makes an announcement to our group. We are to bring our blankets, which are not washed on a weekly basis like the sheets, down to the laundry room during morning tea.

The feeling of these spontaneous alterations when doing this exercise is that help is coming from outside. Each change seems connected to Mr. B's explanation about Will and the quality of how Decisions present themselves or are revealed to us.

A third aspect that is different about Mr. B's version of Decision is evaluating at the end of the day how the task had gone. Only then are we ready to plan the next day's Decision. If we have not done the Decision of the current day and it can still be fulfilled, we are to do it immediately. If it cannot be done because some critical component is no longer available such as daylight or lunchtime, we are to give the body a reminder.

Students keep referring to the reminder as *punishment*, and Mr. B persists in correcting us. Regardless, we find it very difficult to see reminding the body as a positive reinforcement. Holding our arms out for ten minutes isn't the only possible reminder but we can't let go of that image. A friend tells me she dislikes the idea so much that she refuses to recognize the 'reminder' as part of the exercise. What bothers me about the example of holding out one's arms is that it has the grim intensity that so often permeates the methods of the school.

I have failed to do my Decision Exercise today. I cannot remember even thinking about a Decision last night or asking about it this morning. I choose that my reminder will be to carry out two undertakings tomorrow. One is to buy stamps and mail an audiotape letter to Robin, the priest who'd told me about Sherborne; and the other is to clean the dorm fireplace and bring in wood for it.

After Morning Exercise and before we stand for the rukus, I ask about the mailing. I get a 'yes' along with a clear image of handing someone else the money and having that person mail the tape for me. But I think, that would be cheating, wouldn't it? I take 'yes' to just mean 'yes' and ignore the image.

After breakfast, I go up to the dorm where several of us are changing into work clothes. My roommate Amber announces that she is going to the Post Office, an activity not condoned when we're supposed to be going to practical work. She asks if anyone needs anything. I can't resist. I hand her the money, and she mails the audiotape for me. Hadn't the Universe been trying to tell me that's how it would happen?

Later in the morning, as I walk through the courtyard from the garden, I begin picking up stray pieces of wood without giving it any thought. Oliver, the postmaster's terrier, has been pulling them out of the woodpile during his relentless crusade for rats. The wood reminds me about the second task that had, in fact, slipped my mind. I gather up additional wood from the place I intended. When bringing it into the room, I remember that cleaning ashes from the fireplace is also part of the project. It feels like I'm receiving reminders to help me fulfill my intentions.

After weeks of practicing the Decision Exercise, many of us feel like it provides a tone of order to the whole day, the way an orchestra tunes to A before practicing or performing.

WE CANNOT ESCAPE REMEMBERING THE IMPORTANT THINGS THAT HAVE HAPPENED, AND WE CANNOT ESCAPE THE AWARENESS OF THE IMPORTANT THINGS THAT HAVE NOT HAPPENED.

Ralph Salisbury, Cherokee

13 ❧ AND THE HIGHS OF CONNECTION

*Creative activity is never without this taste of delight,
and of course also the taste of surprise and unexpect-
edness, because if it were not surprising and unexpected, it would be something coming from the past.*

JG Bennett

In keeping with the do-it-ourselves prototype, Saturday evenings are a rare opportunity to return to a childhood world where we provide our own entertainment by performing for each other. Afraid to sing in public? Here is a captive audience just like family. A trio plays medieval music on recorders and drum; one time, Linda and Mr. B sing opera; Allen plays Beethoven; Bob recites poetry. I sometimes hear students rehearsing music at lunch or see Jon, who looks like Harlequin, juggling on the lawn at teatime for practice.

As much as I value the concept, I do not attend Saturday evening but a few times; it is the one occasion during the week we are allowed to disregard the schedule without repercussions. Saturday night provides a seemingly unlimited amount of social time to spend with others to do whatever we choose, such as NOTHING! I love that. Patrick and I often hang out with a few of our classmates and then go off for some time alone.

Just as we are expected to provide our own Saturday entertainment, something reflecting the same concept is applied to our daily life. Mr. Bennett tells us many times, "There is no excuse for boredom." He points out that one way we create boredom is when we are not willing to do something we don't already know how to do, be it games, tasks, or inner work. Willingness to experiment reawakens a childlike pleasure in learning that I'd almost forgotten—what I must have been like before I became inhibited by competition, worried about grades, or hungry for recognition.

Even household duties can be transformed. First, it happens by accident, as when changing the pattern of sweeping makes it so interesting that I lose track of time, or going along with a work partner's way of doing a task gives it a new twist, or when prayer makes the chopping of vegetables do double duty by also changing my state.

At Sherborne, claiming boredom is unacceptable. It's not anyone else's job to entertain us. This is our own responsibility to ourselves. In the society outside, playing and discovery are not good enough reasons for doing things. We seem to need a degree to be considered qualified. We don't sing just for the pleasure of it, paint for the enjoyment of looking at colors, or play an instrument just to make interesting sounds. Despite Sherborne's somber and regimented schedule, the ideals demand a creativity that, at least in my schooling, was not much valued.

Not all our serious work is devoid of playfulness. While Patrick, Betty, bespectacled Malcolm of York, and I are creating a massive compost heap, Malcolm says something about compost, but for the life of me, I can't understand a word he's said.

When I tell him, Betty agrees, "Neither did I."

Then Patrick says, "Me neither."

Our long-suffering companion rolls his eyes and repeats what might have been Pigeon English being spoken to lip readers,

"It's—too—bad—we—can't—grind—the—leaves—be-fore—com-post-ing—them.—It—would—help—them—de-com-pose."

I tell him that there have been times since meeting him when I couldn't tell whether he was saying 'yes' or 'no.' "You seem to have a different accent from the other Brits."

"Oh, yes," he answers. "You may not believe it, but I've been modifying my speech the whole time I've been here." Then pointing to Betty, he adds, "Even the English can't understand a Yorkshire accent."

Patrick and Betty reach out at the same time to pat him on the back as if to say, "There, there," causing us all to laugh. We stand for another moment smiling at each other, then, as if there had been an unspoken signal, turn away facing the various directions where each of us had been raking leaves.

A few minutes later Patrick stops and calls to us, pointing to a new pile he's created. "They're like gifts from the trees! We collect them and use them for compost. Nothing is wasted." We murmur in agreement as he opens his arms wide. Crouching down, he gathers up as many leaves as he can and then stands up to release them to the heap, his sweater now decorated with red, orange, and yellow debris.

All four of us lift the heavy wooden gate that serves as the front of the compost enclosure. After we slip it into vertical slots that hold it in place, I leap atop the pile to stomp the leaves down. Swayed by the beauty of the landscape and the warmth of my companions, I shout, "This is our heap!" And as an afterthought, I add, "I'm living in England and loving it!" My buddies are all standing there, leaning on their rakes and grinning at my heartfelt babble.

That's how it is. Classes and lectures full of dark admonitions punctuated by highs of connection.

After dinner, Patrick gives me a back treatment and, once again, I melt under his touch. I feel enveloped by him, as if in a dream, like a floating baby, tiny and protected. His gentle hands skim up my spine, stopping at each chakra—the vortices of energy in the subtle body according to Hindu philosophy. When he strokes my back, tense behind my heart, I surprise myself by bursting into tears. He calls it the compassion chakra and says that the tightness there is from grief.

In late November, we get our first day off after what seems like an eternity since the course began. English colleges call the days off an exeat. At Sherborne, it is usually one day off. The Latin word adds to my monastic impression of Sherborne. I'm thrilled that Patrick has invited me to go with him to Bristol near the western coast where we can walk the beach along an ocean inlet. By this time, we've already decided several times over to just remain friends. I'm not ready for a sexual relationship though I still want to be with him, attracted to his robust self-confidence.

The country roads make the fifty-mile bus ride to Bristol take almost twice as long as we expect from our experiences on American highways. Nevertheless, we are content to sit leaning into each other as we watch the pristine landscape glide past. By the time we arrive, however, the sunny day has become biting cold and blustery. The sky is gray, and the whipping sand makes it painful to walk along the shore.

Instead, we turn to the high street and wander in and out of tourist shops, a dreary activity that causes us to grumble at each other. Only the illustrated postcards of animals at high tea and picnics keep me from sinking into a full funk. The weather continues to reflect our deteriorating moods.

Patrick lets me know that he thinks my agreement to go out with him for the day means that I have changed my mind about sex. When I reiterate my stand, his expression hardens and his face becomes red.

"*Now* you tell me."

It's not as if we had discussed this as a prelude to the trip. I feel torn again by being attracted to him on one hand and wanting done with him on the other. His changing moods frighten me. Thinking, however, that maybe my own moodiness is not that different from his, I say to him, "We're so much alike . . . "

"We are not!"

"Why do you say that?"

"*You* always have to argue with me."

On the awkward return bus ride that afternoon, long after the time we think we should have arrived at Sherborne, we ask the driver when he thinks we'll be coming to it. He tells us that we already passed the village a few towns back. Why hadn't either of us recognized it? We decide we better get off at the next stop and hitchhike back. It should be easy, but it's dusk and there's no traffic at all. It's almost as blustery here as on the beach; then it begins to rain, and we learn the buses have stopped running.

We need to find a room. The inn on the high street has a vacancy; but they have no phone for us to call the school to let them know where we are. We're hungry, too. So steeling ourselves against the bitter weather we go out again in search of a call box. There's one near a restaurant down the street. The operator in Sherborne, however, has no listing for Sherborne House or the International Academy for Continuous Education, IACE the acronym, or J.G. Bennett. We stare at each other dumbfounded. It's like being in a *Twilight Zone* episode. All that we believe to be real is unknown by anyone.

It takes awhile to figure it out. The clue comes from neither of us recognizing the names of any of the towns we've just ridden through. We'd been put on the wrong bus, sent in the opposite direction to another village named Sherborne in the shire of Dorset.

"They sent us to the wrong Sherborne," Patrick says through gritted teeth. Patrick and I had specifically told the ticket seller we were going to Sherborne in Gloucestershire. Did he intentionally misdirect us?

With a phone call made to the correct Sherborne and food in our bellies, we anticipate some warmth and rest. Back at the inn, however, we find the door locked and ringing the bell doesn't rouse anyone. We rush back to the restaurant hoping it's still open. It isn't that late—just a little after nine—yet it wouldn't be unusual in a little village like this for it to be closed by now. One bit of luck. It's still open and the restaurant owner, knowing the innkeeper, phones him on our behalf.

At the lodge, the room is as cold as it is outside. Even though we're dressed and covered with blankets, if it weren't for Patrick's body heat, I doubt I could look forward to sleeping at all. In his anger or maybe just being cold and tired himself, Patrick has nothing more to say about our non-existent sex life.

Although it had taken us less than a couple of hours to get to Bristol, it adds up to twenty-five hours for us to return. Patrick and I sit in the bus, upright and silent as tombstones. The villages look beautiful and exotic, the hills jungle green from the recent rain. I feel Patrick's tension within my own body, fearing his anger. Maybe I can sense other feelings, too, but anger is what I grew up thinking I had to notice. This sensitivity must be how Patrick feels people around him. It's probably how he gives such insightful massages.

Back at Sherborne, no one says anything to us that indicates they noticed our absence, and I embrace the busy schedule in hope of soothing my battered emotions. Although Patrick's aloofness over the next few days amplifies my recurring sense of longing, we achieve a more comfortable distance again. We still spend time together occasionally.

One afternoon during tea, he offers to work on my back, which I strained again bending over in the garden. I'm lying on his bed, and close my eyes to enjoy his warm touch. As he moves his hand across my left scapula, an image of an unknown but familiar street corner appears to me. It doesn't seem to be somewhere I've actually been. Maybe it's a combination of familiar places. There's a wide stone stairway—an eerie silence in a location that's usually bustling with people. First, I remember a dream I had almost every night in my childhood, of falling down a flight of stairs as I was falling asleep. Then comes an image from the movie, *Battleship Potemkin*. I am one of the dead on wide steps that lead down to the harbor where a massacre took place. Patrick is lifting my head. It's as if someone has just found my body and is examining me. Is she alive? What do such images mean?

We stay in Patrick's room so long that we miss our next class. Feeling guilty over my absence, I go to Movements an extra time the next day. In my mind, it is a matter of fulfilling my obligation rather than making up for something I'm sorry to have missed.

Patrick and I aren't as detached as we intend to be. When neither of us can bear the ongoing misunderstandings, and I continue to be adamant about not having sex, he makes what sounds like a final pronouncement; "You'll be my sister from now on."

What a relief, I think, to be rid of at least one pressure.

> THE ABILITY TO DELUDE YOURSELF MAY
> BE AN IMPORTANT SURVIVAL TOOL.
>
> *Jane Wagner*

14 ∾ CLOISTERED

> *The dullness of the world all comes from our own dull state, because we are just not seeing the world in which we are.*
>
> *JG Bennett*

The unyielding schedule marches on, workdays making a clearer impression on me than class days. It is mostly during work that I have personal conversations and find out in an informal way what other people are experiencing.

Tomás, who is part Native American, and I have already mucked out the chicken coop, fought off the attack rooster, and fed everyone. I must have collected about three-dozen eggs, pleased with the intimacy of feeling the soft warm bellies of the laying hens. After delivering water and hay to the donkeys, we rest a moment out in the field, leaning on the fence and staring up at the Georgian estate. It doesn't seem quite as squat as it appeared at first.

Tomás has dark hair and eyes but his appearance contains nothing gruff about it. He's easy to be with. I've heard he sings and speaks several languages. Pointing out the church connected to the building, Tomás asks, "Have you ever been inside?"

"Only once." I answer, thinking of Morgan's midnight mass. "Do they still use it?"

"Every Sunday. It's the village church." He starts walking toward it. "It's almost teatime. Let's take a detour on the way."

Tomás is a fount of information. He seems to know something about everything, always contributing to any discussions when there's a question to be answered. He explains to me that it was typical for the owner of a large estate to provide a place of worship for the local people.

Inside the church, it is cold and dank with several sculptures of saints stationed around the room. The pews have cross-stitched cushions on them. Even at thirty I still haven't gotten used to seeing a man nailed to a cross to symbolize the religion of love. A few years before, a dream softened the horror of it by a dancing Shiva superimposed over the cross. Shiva destroying attachments to the material world by treading on them was more compatible with my heart.

"You know," Tomás says, "this estate was constructed around an earlier monastery."

"It was?"

I tell him how back in Chicago I kept telling my friends that I was going to a monastery, though Bennett never called it that in any of his printed materials.

Tomás tells me that his roommate Shaun had gotten a psychic reading before coming to Sherborne. "You will be returning to the monastery where you'd once been a monk," the psychic told him. Tomás, too, has strange feelings about Sherborne as a monastery. That's how he and Shaun had come to discuss it.

We stand awhile without talking. Inside my head, I am watching men in robes walking through gardens, passing each other without speaking, then filing into the pews of a dark church. Maybe Tomás is watching the same scene. Could we students know each other from a past life?

I flinch when Tomás's voice breaks my reverie. "You know the stone room with the pillars near the staircase to the Bennett's apartment? It's a cloister from the monastery."

I nod, " . . . oh, it never occurred to me—a real cloister. . . ."

"Let's walk through it, too."

"It's my favorite part of the building," I tell him. "It never dawned on me it had been built earlier than the rest of the house."

We step out the side door of the church directly into Sherborne House and walk a short distance down the hall to the cloister. What had once been an outdoor courtyard surrounded by a columned covered walkway is now embedded within the building. The walls and floor are stone and its location makes it somewhat dark, yet I've always found it serene and inviting.

I tell Tomás, "It has its own feeling, and I'm often drawn to dawdling here when I'm working in this end of the house."

"The kitchen is also part of the monastery," Tomás says. "Several of us have been breaking through one of the walls that has an old bread-baking oven hidden behind it."

Ah, the pick axes I saw students carrying . . .

Looking down at the stone floor we're standing on, it's easy to see places where it's worn smooth by at least a couple of centuries' worth of footsteps. It dips in the doorways.

I'm happy Tomas and I are in the same group because it means we are in the same classes and often share duties. But it is usually Mick I associate with unexpected surprises. I don't know how he fulfills his staff obligations and still provides so many students with a sense of personal relationship and delightful escapades. I know I'm not the only one accruing Mick stories. Maybe it's because in contrast to Mr. B's other old students, it feels like he's accepting and respectful even when he disagrees with you and points to the possibility of seeing things differently.

On another day, the whole student body piles into a rented bus to attend a Mevlevi performance in a large auditorium in London. I'm under the impression that Mick is the instigator of our attending the event. These are the whirling dervishes as they are referred to in popular vernacular. The music and turning are deeply affecting. At certain moments, energy shoots out of the dancers, blasting us, though we're seated some distance from the stage. I'm uncomfortable—as if this is a ritual I'm not supposed to be seeing. Perhaps my reaction speaks to our observing an actual practice, not a performance, and I wonder why it's being made public.

Pushing my discomforts out of my mind, I am left instead to contemplate the awesome feeling I have toward Mick for having packed each of us a brown bag dinner that we ate on the bus as we drove to London.

Mick leads me toward the garden where he's going to point out kale to pick for dinner. Next to the tool shed and the woodpile is a building that looks like an old garage. "Gerald Wilde lives there," Mick tells me.

"Someone lives there? Who is he?"

"He's an old painter. Did you ever see the movie, *The Horse's Mouth*?"

"I *have.*"

"Well, Gulley Jimson, the hero, was modeled after Gerald!"

Mick says that some people describe Gerald as a lunatic, but he's known in the art world as the only British abstract expressionist. I hadn't read Joyce Carey's novel, but in the movie, Jimson has a continuous stream of outrageous adventures, all for the sake of Art. In one scene he breaks into a rich couple's apartment while they're on vacation to paint a mural on their perfect wall. The next great artwork he executes is on the remaining wall of a decrepit church about to be demolished. Jimson gets helpers to paint sections of the mural under the guise of giving them painting lessons. He has each one copy from a paper on which he's painted a segment of his composition. It is a monumental work that Jimson's admirers decide they will fight to preserve. They gather on the intended day of razing to have a standoff with the authorities. In the end, the wall comes crashing down. When the dust clears, it is Jimson himself who is driving the bulldozer. He makes a statement. "Too great a responsibility, destroying a masterpiece, to allow the demolition crew to do it."

"Why is Gerald living at Sherborne House?" I ask Mick while he knocks on the door.

"Mr. B thinks he's a genius. He just wants to help him out. Those are his works hanging on the wall in the ballroom."

"Oh, those are *his* abstract paintings. They seem like lunacy only in contrast to the stiff plaster and crystal chandelier. I love their bold clean lines."

Just then, Gerald pokes his head out the garage door and, before he can retreat, Mick introduces us. We give each other a wary eye and then Gerald vanishes back into his den, muttering about having been tricked into socializing.

The following weekend, I happen to bump into Gerald at the post office. Feeling awkward about trying to converse, I say, "I enjoy those paintings of yours in the ballroom."

"They're shit!" he answers, and then buys me a grapefruit, which I'm delighted to have, as I can't remember the last time I ate fresh fruit. This must be his way of balancing being irascible, but I have no more clarity about him than about the rest of the activities at Sherborne.

Later in the day, I'm checking the wooden pigeonholes in the hall near the kitchen where we pick up our mail. There's a long cardboard tube Gerald has left for me. In it is a beautiful close-up photograph of Mr. B and Gerald with the corner of one of Gerald's paintings peeking out of the background. The photo is almost a foot square and in color. Dissociating from my receiving such a special memento, I register it as if I'm watching the scene from afar, and with the sense that it's not Gerald's response to me but the result of Mick's introduction.

While personal interactions punctuate the days, most of our time is still filled with scheduled studies and tasks. Morning Exercise continues to grow in complexity. In our heads we are repeating a short prayer in English while in our chests we say the same in Russian. At the same time, we sense our limbs in a pattern of one after another, skipping a different limb each time around. Every exercise we do stretches the ability to direct attention. While they mostly feel beyond my capacity, I can tell at other times that making the effort is improving my ability to concentrate.

I'm always hungry for warm moments of companionship, and although I find them, abrupt reminders to remember myself still often jolt me.

For a couple of months, I have been trying to accustom myself to sitting on a cushion but my joints and back always draw more of my attention than Morning Exercise. I never choose to sit on a chair, not wanting to be 'self-indulgent' or 'weak,' to use the words that are bandied about here. I finally have the temerity to sit on a bench. Paula, the woman who was given dispensation to talk on silent days, marches over to me.

"These are only for people who have back problems!"

Despite years of tribulations with my back, doctors telling me my last option is surgery, she shames me and I return to a cushion believing that somehow she knows who is hurting more. After all, I don't have my x-rays with me to prove anything to her. Anyone speaking with conviction can intimidate me, and I always find a way to ignore the voice inside.

> YOU ARE ALWAYS ONLY ONE CHOICE
> AWAY FROM CHANGING YOUR LIFE.
>
> *Marcy Blochowiak*

15 ❧ A KICK IN THE SHINS

> *Feeling is that power which enables us to have contact with a higher level.*
>
> *JG Bennett*

"We're trying to accumulate energy here, and you're a leak!"

Almost every time I am playful or laugh, someone, student or staff, proclaims that I'm dissipating energy, sometimes mine, sometimes that of the entire school. Mr. B never says this to me personally, though he speaks of the concept in our group meetings. I *can* feel a depletion of energy when I complain, but laughter or play usually increases it. Experience just doesn't match what I am told with such certainty by others. It's one more incongruity that adds to my confusion.

Another source of perplexity that *does* come from Mr. B is his use of language. It includes a mixture of his and Gurdjieff's recognizable and obscure words—buffers, hyparxis, self-indulgence, hazard, transformation, demiurge, and more. Take the word 'experience', a word that I think I comprehend in the way he uses it. Yet when I look it up in one of his book glossaries, the definition is, "The total givenness possible for all and every consciousness, human, sub-human and super-human. The definite form of the indefinite reality." I just have to hope I am looking at a definition taken out of context.

His language is always stretching my ability to comprehend anything he says. All of these words have exact meanings, explaining tl ˙ workings of the universe as he sees it. When I can concentrate on his explanations during lectures, I am astonished by how he describes every-day experiences such as 'needing excuses for bad behavior' in an almost mathematical yet qualitative way. Still, no matter how awe-inspiring his language, it does not appear to improve communication among the people around me.

I never ask questions that might make Mr. B's concepts more comprehensible. After all, there are people at Sherborne who have studied with him for years and *they* understand what he's saying. I would have to interrupt so often he'd never make it through a lecture. Besides, in the end, I have little interest in pursuing so much complexity of thought.

The way Mr. B and our teachers speak about human behavior feels hopeless. Based on Gurdjieff's teachings, man is asleep. He cannot do. Man is a machine. He once had an organ called Kundabuffer the results of which became crystallized and continues to prevent him from perceiving correctly. Though Gurdjieff's explanation is said in a manner that makes me laugh, I all too easily see mankind this way. What I need is how to find our strengths, how to see difficulties from a positive, yet not naïve, point of view.

In my life, the experience of coming to greater discernment usually occurs from real life encounters that give me a sense of the wounded child still living within an adult. Observing kindness and humor or seeing inclusiveness in situations where it is unexpected often causes me to give a second thought to my impatience, anger, giving up, or other limiting behavior. The shock of compassion is what awakens in me the wish to change.

"This way of working isn't for everyone," Mr. B and his staff tell us students fairly often. But I hate to think it might not be for me.

At intervals, Mr. Bennett offers a class he calls open discussion. That means we are invited to ask questions about any topic. A couple of people ask about situations where they have to deal with feeling angry or irritated. Mr. B reminds us of the qualities of our reactional self, a part of us that is essentially dualistic in nature.

"If this self is too strong," Mr. B says, "it can be oversensitive and moody. It sees things in black and white, sometimes to the point of being cruel to others. It is a poor master if undisciplined but a good servant when in balance. It is lively and receptive, perceptive with a love of beauty, capable of affection and generosity, able to be logical and clear mentally."

In a rare moment of bravado, I raise my hand to ask Mr. B a question.

"In relation to what Vin and Donna said . . . "

"Can't you speak about yourself?" he barks.

Tears well up from his rebuke, but I manage to breathe through my upset and continue. "At moments of distress or even when something very positive happens, can't we do a blending to use the energy created by the situation?" I am thinking of prayers or how at the end of Movements classes we ask silently that our efforts enter within us, or the way I'm telling myself to keep breathing right now.

"Yes," he says, "The energy can be blended through sensation, by sensing the left leg or the right hand, for example."

I dare a second question because I am still stuck on using words as the method to handle distress.

"Is it done better by sensing than by using words internally?"

"Yes. Sensing is how we remain present. This is how we develop our Being. It is so difficult for Westerners, whereas Asians take it for granted. It's so natural for them to be present, they are mystified by our situation."

While telling myself to breathe again, I'm trying to sort out if I'm remaining present by talking to myself or by attending to the sensation of breathing.

At that meeting, I recognize something more about why the Gestalt workshops I attended years ago had been so life changing. We practiced an exercise called the Continuum of Awareness that engendered increasing our awareness of *how* we experience the present moment, rather than *why* we have the experiences we do.

The gist of the exercise is for the person practicing to describe his awareness. When I am the person working, the one in the so-called 'hot seat' I might say: I'm aware of sitting with my right leg crossed over my left knee. I'm aware of jiggling my right foot. I feel my foot moving up and down. I notice you are watching my jiggling foot. I am aware of thinking that you're thinking I'm stupid for jiggling my foot. I'm aware of my face getting hot from that thought. I'm aware that my arm itches and deciding not to scratch it. I'm aware that I'm thinking you think I'm nervous for jiggling my foot. I'm aware of whispering going on in the back of the room. I'm aware of wondering if they're talking about me. I'm aware of tension in my belly, and so forth.

Doing this exercise many times made me aware of sensations within my body that even years of dancing lessons had never awakened an awareness of. It was crucial for me because it connected me to the habit of suppressing emotions that I was taught I shouldn't have: It's not good to be angry. You shouldn't feel jealous, annoyed, hurt, or superior. However, suppressed emotions have to find a way out and when they did, I didn't know why I couldn't control the resulting behaviors. In ordinary language, the phenomenon is called 'acting out.'

Fritz Perls, the innovator of Gestalt, would remind his students, "Lose your mind and come to your senses." Maybe this is what Mr. B means when he says, "It is not so important to observe what you are feeling as to be able to recognize *how* you are feeling," that is, how we are experiencing the sensations connected to emotional feeling.

Before Gestalt, I might have felt sad without realizing it until days later. When I learned to pay attention to a sensation that I call 'the hollowness in my chest,' I became aware of sadness in the moment it began. Making the connection allows me to find other ways to express myself that I didn't have choices about before. Allowing recognition of sadness, for example, gives me the opportunity to address the reasons for it, whether it is an interaction with a person or the elements of a situation that I can involve or remove myself from.

At Sherborne, emotions are often talked about with contempt, as if they offer little because they are so often expressed unconsciously. Also, they change too much to be depended upon. We are told 'not to identify' with them. "You are not your emotions." This is interpreted by most students as advice to disregard them. Compare ignoring an emotion to taking a pain-numbing drug for a broken bone instead of using the pain as an indicator to get the bone aligned so it can heal properly. Likewise, we learn, "You are not your thoughts," yet we don't interpret that to mean we should stop using our brains just because some ideas are destructive. In meditative practice, we see all these parts of ourselves as just that: parts of a complex and layered picture, none of which equate the whole person.

WHAT YOU ARE LOOKING FOR IS WHAT IS LOOKING.

St Francis of Assisi

I'm appalled when first getting to know George, the husband of Mary, matriarch-of-the-kitchen. He is in his sixties and in charge of the practical work that focuses on construction and maintenance. He has thin graying reddish hair and always dresses in the plaid flannel or khaki shirt of a handy man. Despite his age, he behaves like a childish bully, alternately pouting and bragging.

"On Kodiak Island where I live in Alaska, my cabbages are twice this size," or "How come none of you boys know how to fix that?" In every group conversation, he manages to allude to the fact that he had been a student of Gurdjieff's. At least one person among those working with George at any given moment is rolling his eyes. At first I can barely be civil, my tolerance of him so tenuous.

I am taken aback the first time he asks me to cut his hair, a favorite activity I've been practicing ever since someone found out that I cut my own. Being with George at regular intervals gives me the opportunity to converse with him about ordinary things, not The Fourth Way. I find myself becoming somewhat fond of him despite his childish quirks and the remarkable lack of his awareness of them. My reaction to George is a good example of how feelings can change.

I start cutting hair more than ever. Like running my own sculpture studio. Classmates often surprise me by bestowing a gift in exchange—a bottle of wine, chocolate, or unique objects, like the little yellow button depicting Mr. Natural that Vinnie dug up. And George, that curmudgeon, rewards me with a new haircutting razor.

This is one pending haircut that is failing to inspire joy. Sherry, a single parent, is dragging her seven-year-old son by his upper arm into my room at lunchtime. I don't know the boy, and their hostile exchange sets off a little alarm in my head. His mother forces him to sit in the chair.

"I don't want a haircut!"

"It'll just take a minute," Sherry insists. "Sit there and let her cut your hair."

The final order settles it for him. She isn't listening to him. He leaps out of the chair, spins around, and kicks me in the shin as hard as he can. While I'm hopping around on my good leg and clutching the other knee to my belly, Sherry figures it must be time for them to go. Now I understand why childcare has become the domain for parents and those who pledge unconditional love for kids. Parents say it's to get the best care for their children, but the truth is it's too dangerous for the uninitiated.

LET THE PERSON I SERVE EXPRESS HIS THANKS ACCORDING TO HIS OWN BRINGING UP AND HIS SENSE OF HUMOR.

Charles A. Eastman

Another example of emotions causing turmoil happens whenever someone has been assigned an egregious task or finds himself at odds with another student. The 'victim' credits Mr. B with having personally orchestrated the situation. Do they think Mr. B would need to advise the staff, "Let's drive the compulsively neat kitchen boy over the edge by assigning him to work with a cook who insists upon using every pot and utensil in the kitchen"? Hasn't anyon ever noticed before living at Sherborne that life always accommodates us with a constant flow of challenges?

Patrick and I are still in the same group together, and not all of our encounters are bad. Today we are serving breakfast and I fuss about whether we'll be able to get everything done in time for our next activity. He rests his hand on my left arm, stopping me in my tracks, as I think he's about to say something. Instead, he moves his hand to my back for just a moment while I allow myself awareness of its warmth. All of my muscles relax, one by one, up and down my spine, my shoulders, my hands, as if by their own accord. I hadn't realized how tense they'd become. His relaxed touch soothes my body and my mind follows suit. I value what Patrick is showing me, and I want to share with him a related experience I've had, but he cuts me off.

"It isn't the same thing," he says before I've even completed a sentence.

This often happens when I venture to compare something I've learned outside of Sherborne. He behaves as if a concept experienced elsewhere would diminish the uniqueness of the Work. Patrick, too, disparages psychology as a subject having nothing to do with spirituality. Experience showed me that spirituality is a natural urge of human development. In general, psychology is a dirty word here unless it refers to Sherborne's psychology class. Patrick is angry about an encounter group he experienced years ago. Maybe it was confrontational or hostile. He never would let me tell him about what I'd experienced. The mere mention of Gestalt psychology would start him ranting.

"All that indulgence in feelings just intensifies them. It doesn't release them."

He must have experienced a facilitator who was either unsympathetic or unable to help people complete the process. As easily intimidated as I am, I'd never had a bad experience with Gestalt. Instead, despite my still being a work in progress, before coming here I learned a lot about layers of suppressed feelings, how to unscramble them and, best of all, how to experiment with using them. But Patrick will never hear me through on this topic. It's perplexing to see him get so agitated over it.

What a conundrum—trying to integrate what I value at Sherborne with what I know from my past. I am being told, on one hand, that my experiences don't count while on the other hand, Mr. B expects me to verify whether the events at Sherborne are serving the aim I've determined for myself.

16 ❧ NOTHING THAT IS SOMETHING

If we wish to serve, we must know that we cannot do it as long as we remain as we are. We have to change.

JG Bennett

"What's wrong with you Americans? Just what do you find so difficult about making a pot of tea?" April, who is in charge of serving tea in the dining room this morning, is angry with me for having made the brew too weak. She grabs the pot out of my hands and whisks it off to the servery.

I used the amount of leaves she'd told me to, and I run after her, disgusted with her haranguing. "Why not just show me the ideal strength? Why do you have to be so negative?" She jerks to a halt, clenching her teeth. Like a chameleon, her face slowly fills with color changing it from London chalk to chilblain pink as she continues to glare at me.

"I . . . I am NOT negative!" she bellows.

I stand for a moment, wide-eyed, taking in her contorted expression, then turn and walk away. To my surprise, laughter wells up from deep inside and bursts through the barrier I try to create with my lips. I guess that laughing instead of creeping away admonished must be a kind of breakthrough for me. The next morning I awaken with the following dream lingering in my head:

> I am washing the face of a little baby and admiring how tiny and pretty it is. My heart is overflowing with love as I talk to it. When it speaks with me, I tell it how intelligent it is, too. It thanks me and tells me how it has just finished college. I think, This baby must be a sort of genius!

AN EFFECTIVE WAY TO DEAL WITH
PREDATORS IS TO TASTE TERRIBLE.

Unknown

As often as scenes like the one with April offend me, just as frequently I get to see the other side of the coin. On kitchen duty, the chief cook assigns me to chop garlic for dinner. I cut the end off the first of seven cloves and pick away at the thin peel that is difficult to separate from the meat. Mary is on her way over. I can see she's intending to correct something I'm doing, and I'm determined to fend her off.

"I can do it," I say before she opens her mouth.

She talks over my protests. "If you crush the clove with the handle of the knife, the skin just pops off."

Always ready to fight criticism, at least I back off this time and try what she suggests. Her technique works perfectly. I'm able to get the skin off the rest of the cloves in less time than I'd already spent struggling with the first. When will I tire of feeling I've got to prove my competence without anyone's help?

When Mr. B introduces a new theme—bodies—it feels apropos to all our daily struggles with *doing* in the form of Decisions and practical work. He presents the concept of bodies as a duality we always face.

"The body is our prison or our path. We can become caught up and dominated by it, or it can be the medium through which we find our creative spiritual potential. Through matter we can learn lessons that lead to an expansion of spirit, of love."

When Mr. B speaks in this way, his belief in another approach to *being* is palpable. It confirms all the spiritual traditions that describe Earth as a school where with intention we can learn lessons that only material existence provides. Before Sherborne, reading about reincarnation suggested to me for the first time that I could benefit from life's difficulties and that we are given learning moments as often as we need them. The idea that there is more to life than getting good grades and making a good living gives me a sense of purpose I cannot otherwise muster.

Mr. Bennett talks about observing ourselves in relation to the material world, noticing such attitudes as greed, punishment, and retribution. He explains how the material world demonstrates the results of our way of thinking. In the protected environment of Sherborne, as irritating as it can be, I value the endless opportunities we have to observe ourselves taking unfair portions of food, avoiding work, acting like despots when in a position of power, and being unpleasant or pleasant for personal gain.

THIS IS THE FIRST LESSON YE SHOULD LEARN:
THERE IS SO MUCH GOOD IN THE WORST OF US,
AND SO MUCH BAD IN THE BEST OF US, IT DOESN'T
BEHOOVE ANY OF US TO SPEAK EVIL OF THE REST OF US.

Edgar Cayce

Gertie, a 42-year-old woman in my group, has short dark hair that curls around her friendly face. Despite the difference in our ages and the fact that she's already raised a family, we find each other sympathetic company. Whenever we have the opportunity, we chat about our perceptions of Sherborne. After another disheartening lecture, Gertie says, "I was in Mrs. Popoff's study group before coming here. The Work as she teaches it is much gentler. It wasn't like this." The authority of her experience bolsters me. She has a more balanced attitude about everything despite or maybe because of the challenges in her life. Gertie knows she has Parkinson's disease though I can't tell. Her hands don't shake at all.

"If you watch me when I'm doing Movements you'll see I can no longer raise my arms vertically. I've already made plans. I'm making payments to a Quaker community up in New York that offers comprehensive nursing care." I admire her ability to plan her future. I can't imagine her disabled and developing the flat affect that typifies the disease when now her eyes crinkle with laughter as we joke together.

Esther, Gertie's daughter, is here with her. She's about twenty years old and a very slow learner. Esther doesn't much like Sherborne, mostly because it's so cold and, as she has told me, "The teachers are mean." She's figured that out from their unsmiling demands about how the housework or cooking should be done. Esther's been invited to participate in any of the activities that interest her. Most often she chooses to work in the kitchen. It's the only warm room in the building for one thing, and help with food preparation and cleanup is always appreciated.

Another place where Esther and I meet even more often is next to the cryptic radiator at the stairway near our rooms, the only one in the building that I know of, though this doesn't make sense. With her shoulders hunched against the cold and wearing her pale yellow or green handmade sweater Esther often knits while leaning against the bare radiator fins. She holds her project down at her side when chatting with students as we make our way to classes or chores. When we feel down, we complain to her, knowing she'll support our sentiments. Indeed, her lack of rationalization is refreshing.

One evening, the school holds an anniversary memorial dinner for Mr. Gurdjieff who had died in 1949. I'm on my way to the dorm afterward when Gertie asks if I'll put her glasses in her room. She's going to stay downstairs. When I get to the room, Esther is there looking as if she's about to burst into tears. I walk over and put my arms around her, and we both start crying.

Then she tells me why.

"The service reminds me of my father," she says. "He died six years ago."

Gertie and Esther had both told me about Esther's spiritual longing, and I wonder if she, like the rest of us driven to Sherborne, is missing a *spiritual* father, not only the biological one.

A third of the way through the ten-month course, just when I'm sure one more day of house duty is going to send me over the edge, my gloomy mood takes on a strange equanimity. Our a.m. service team finishes breakfast cleanup much earlier than usual. This allows me to devote an hour-and-a-half to my Decision Exercise that involves the houseplants I enjoy so much. Late in the morning, I realize that our team hasn't cut bread for lunch. I don't bother to look for any of the other servers with whom the duty is ordinarily shared; I just cut the twelve loaves myself, still having plenty of time to spare.

When I glance out the window of the dining hall, I see a lone figure rushing through the park-like sheep field. It's Pierre, our Movements and gardening teacher, running once again, perhaps on his way to finish up some task before lunch. He loses his footing on the lawn and slides to a perfect landing on his belly. At this distance I can't hear him cry out nor does it look as if he did. He just picks himself up and, with no loss of momentum, launches full steam ahead like a ship on its maiden voyage. I stand awhile, arms crossed, my mouth open, bemused at seeing him fall once again.

In the afternoon, my assignment is working by myself—ironing, using the mangle to press bed sheets. Being alone most of the day is such a relief that the whole day has become the opposite of what I'd been dreading. Maybe it isn't the work I resist as much as the constant companionship.

For a few days, I drift into reveries about Voltaire's *Candide*, a book I'd read years ago. Recalling its un-ambitious ending brings me comfort. The characters, after lives of death defying

NOTHING THAT IS SOMETHING ❦ 137

strife, retire to live together in a cottage, and tend their garden. My urbane friends in Chicago found it shocking when I advanced the attractiveness of this image. Perhaps they thought I was too young to be promoting such dullness.

Now, a small package arrives for me—an audiotape letter from Robin, the priest in Chicago. In one of those well-timed moments, Robin says, "Everything's so chaotic here. I wish we were just living in a charming little cottage and gardening together."

Until now, Mr. B's references to energy have been understandable, though hinting of a greater meaning—where energies have different qualities and can be used intentionally to create change. He presents the subject of 'Energies' as a Theme for observation as well as a topic for a series of lectures.

"By understanding energies," he says, "we can learn to use them. Transformation is an integral fact of the entire universe whether we're talking about the mechanics of physics, the quality of life for human and other living beings, or cosmic elements beyond human life."

His words remind me of my motivation for having come to Sherborne in the first place, something I keep forgetting while trudging through the endless motions of our routine—wake up, swear about the dirty tubs, try to keep warm, ache from sitting on the floor, make Decisions, change from muddy work clothes, eat meals, wash dishes, sweep, go to class, Movements, Movements, Movements. Meanwhile, Mr. B's complex and sensitive lectures wash over me like the tides. Unlike those who thrive on the multifaceted intellectual systems, the more time we spend in that heady world, the more life feels dull and incomplete.

But the talks on Energy draw me in. Mr. B says, "Energy gives rise to all that exists, beginning with the material world, moving up through energies that stand on the threshold of life, such as viruses, then life and the growth of living things, awareness, the development of consciousness, and culminating with the higher powers of the cosmos beyond human life."

I never before understood how all these things are connected to each other. Using a chart, he describes a continuum of twelve distinct energies, how every kind of energy can be transformed into the type of energy above it or below it by adding or taking away a quality.

The chart also paints a literal picture of Mr. B's explanation that those who have developed an understanding or ability to do something have an obligation to help those who have not. At whatever level or in whatever the subject, taking action is a way for man to continue to create the world, not merely occupy a place in it.

ONCE YOU CAN ACCEPT THE UNIVERSE
AS MATTER EXPANDING INTO NOTHING THAT IS SOMETHING,
WEARING STRIPES WITH PLAID COMES EASY.

Albert Einstein

A visiting instructor named Hugo teaches a class called Hermeneutics. We meet in the airy upstairs library where we always have tea after eating lunch. The light from the long windows eases our introduction to this arcane subject. Hermeneutics is the science of interpretation, usually referring to scripture. In this case, though, it is the interpretation of life. Hugo calls the Hermeneutic encounter a wholesome encounter. Though the class makes sense to me while in the midst, I doubt I can explain it to anyone. I leave each meeting with snippets and a strong feeling. Hermeneutics conveys a sense of what it means to be 'in the flow.' I don't claim that Hugo said the following, only that these notions are what I am left with when we finish the class:

- Talking about anything isn't the same as experiencing it.
- In truth, there are no subjects and verbs. Experience is more like the mutuality or synchronicity of the makings of an event.

Hugo describes how we try to catch language in the act. "We try to describe what makes an event by speaking it, not speaking *about* it; and when all the circumstances are right, language flows, discloses, sees, says, shows the truth." I imagine this is like the way expository prose speaks *about* experience while poetry, which often is illogical and ungrammatical, confers something of the experience of the object or moment being described.

During another session Hugo quotes St. Francis, "What you are looking for is what is doing the looking." He tells us how the personality is always trying to interfere and own the stream.

Vinnie, the quirky New York music journalist says, "The personality is like a bank teller who is happy to be so generous about giving you your own money."

Hugo adds. "The personality tries to take over or take credit because when the event happens, it is more real than you are. The experience is reality."

Over the weeks, Hugo continues trying to move us into our experiences. He talks about the noun and verb structure where the verb is held secondary to the noun, interfering with our understanding the process. "Grass is green," was another example Hugo used, "as if you could separate these things. Grass is grassing or grassing is greening might be more accurate. The limit of my language is the limit of my world," he says.

Vinnie gets it. He always brings all topics around to music. "When you hear the melody, you have to believe the lyrics," he says.

What I hear is how the form of our language, English, sets us up for falling into duality and separation. No wonder I value silence.

LANGUAGE EXERTS HIDDEN POWER,
LIKE A MOON ON THE TIDES.

Rita Mae Brown

17 ∾ UP AND DOWN
AND ALL AROUND

You don't matter a bit as something separate from
everything else. No, you only matter because you're
connected with everything. You have to keep putting
this right in yourself.

JG Bennett

American students are asking for a Thanksgiving celebration.
The English tease Americans about Thanksgiving—as if the holiday is the only time during the year it occurs to us to be thankful.

We have a gentle Thanksgiving dinner. The group on house
duty has created a festive atmosphere. Decorations materialize
from nowhere. The landscape around the estate is wintry, not at
all lush, yet they fill tall vases with dried grasses from the fields
and set colorful autumn squashes on the tables along with every
living houseplant in the building. Patterned Indian bedspreads,
from any of us who owns one, cover the tables.

Mr. Bennett, still wearing his hound's tooth coat, announces
that George, our maintenance expert, has told him it is traditional
in America for the old man of the house, in this case referring
to Mr. B, to say something at the dinner table. He asks us if that
is so, as if he can't quite trust George's word. We conspire with
George or, perhaps, it's true. My father or grandfathers never
gave a speech, though it's often shown that way in the movies or
on TV. Mr. Bennett graciously proceeds to speak about his own
heritage, one parent English and one American and welcomes all
of us to celebrate this special dinner.

Patrick invites me to dine with him, that is, to sit next to him on a bench at one of the long decorated tables. After dinner we all do Movements, and after Movements are over at 10 p.m., Patrick and I take an ambling walk on the property.

Not long after Thanksgiving, before morning tea, I walk out to a field where Patrick, wearing a thin blue jean jacket, repairs the fence. The oranges and gold of autumn still gleam, and a flock of white sheep punctuates the long green hill on the other side of the property fence. It is bitter cold and, even with my winter coat, gloves, and scarf, I can't keep my shoulders from hunching up to my ears. Yet Patrick looks perfectly comfortable while taking unusual care with his labors. He greets me with enthusiasm—radiant, glowing with pleasure. He must love being out here.

"What are you doing?" I ask, noting it's past practical work time.

"I've been repairing the fence for the last three days. It's nice to have a visitor."

"It won't be for long. I don't know how you can stand it out here. I'm freezing." Too cold to stay more than a few minutes, I keep moving by gathering a bagful of kindling for the dorm as we talk. "I've got to back," I tell him. "This wind hurts too much."

"I'll see you at tea," he calls to my back.

He shows up at teatime, and we chat about some philosophical ideas and then joke about not arguing. Something is easier between us.

We students have nothing on the schedule for the evening, the only time I can remember that happening. This small freedom, despite my being on house duty, makes the whole day seem like a holiday. When evening comes, Patrick finds me while I finish my stint on p.m. service and tells me he's going to the social club. Although we've not made any plans for the evening, I feel abandoned.

I hear there's going to be a gathering in Lucas' dorm and because I learned about the party by accident, I take it as a sign that I should go. The communal culture here means that every-one is invited whether you receive a personal invitation or not.

Anselm as brewed a gallon of apple cider, the same color as his auburn hair. He explains, or perhaps it is more accurate to say, demonstrates that cider in England is not apple juice but an alcoholic beverage. Its slight bite is not enough to deter one from drinking too much. Not long after the party has gotten under way, Patrick shows up, saying he's just been to my room looking for me. My feeling abandoned puffs into non-existence, and with relish, we leave the party to spend the next few hours talking and cuddling. Each time Patrick and I have a pleasant encounter, I fall headlong into wanting more from him. For him, the lack of sexual expression makes him sullen and irri-table. Yet we still can't finish with each other.

SUCCESS CONSISTS OF GOING FROM FAILURE TO FAILURE WITHOUT LOSS OF ENTHUSIASM.

Winston Churchill

Dick, a frail older man with a gray mustache, a neat part in his hair, and a high square forehead teaches us history and psychol-ogy. He looks as if the suit he wears is ballast keeping him from blowing away in the slightest breeze. In contrast, his blossoming daughter, in her early teens, has rosy cheeks and brims with the energy of youthful promise. Dick always conveys protection and tenderness toward her. She conveys the same for him. She tells me how students come to his door day and night asking for help, and she often falls asleep to the sound of hushed whisperings as he counsels them. Whenever she gets good and tired of their hounding him, if he happens to be in the loo when they come knocking, she tells them he's gone to Cheltenham for the day.

In Dick's class, he has already told us several times about a man who quit smoking. The man was so oblivious to his own habits that he smoked a cigarette while telling someone how he'd quit. Is Dick the man?

Dick also speaks about the English attitude toward revolution. He explains that, instead, they act according to the concept of reform. The idea is to re-do the past, restoring and correcting an activity to bring it up to the standards of some ancient ideal. Is it revolution or reform that is the problem? Despite this uncertainty sticking in my head, I never ask questions to further my understanding.

Bev has the cot next to mine. She often disappears late at night, dragging her sleeping bag and pillow behind her, off for a midnight tryst, I suppose. She's a buoyant girl with dark fuzzy hair, curlier than my own. One of the youngest people at Sherborne, she chooses to make friends of Bennett's students who are either on the staff or who joined the course after having studied at Coombe Springs. She isn't coy about her personality, telling me up front that she loves competing and intentionally sought out Bennett's students with the hope of positioning herself to learn more.

"I don't find them all that enlightened, though," she admits.

She works so hard at everything we are assigned that I'm surprised when she tells me her history. "I used to get into so much trouble that I was sent to high school in an Outward Bound program. I loved it. We lived out in the woods and had to do everything for ourselves."

I've heard of Outward Bound because of my interest in alternative education. They have workshops and compulsory programs for delinquents. I didn't know that they also provided accredited high school. The idea is to challenge students by putting them out in the wild where they need to build shelters, find food, and interact with each other in a way that assures everyone's survival. Bev thrived on the pressure.

Never unpleasant toward me, she, nevertheless, gives me the impression that I serve her no apparent purpose; I'm not in the strata of enlightened society to which she aspires, nor am I a motivating force even for myself, shunning, as I do, anything that hints of competition. Nevertheless, her personality is so different from mine that I delight in hearing her talk about her adventures.

After practical work today, Bev lugs into our dorm a brown cardboard carton about twenty inches in each dimension.

"It's from my mother in Florida," she says, "Probably health food snacks. Stick around, you can have some."

"Really? You'd share it?" I can't believe she's willing to let any of it go. She isn't talking only to me. Our dorm mates gather around the package as if it's a rock star. After picking out a few protein bars for herself, she lets the rest of us choose whatever we want—almonds, cashews, apricot rolls, veggie chips, and other health store snacks. There must be a couple of dozen treats—all dispersed in a matter of seconds. Bev shows an easy relationship with the material world. It was an expensive package to ship, not counting the cost of its contents, and she isn't miserly with the gifts.

Not long afterward, when mail delivery includes a care package for me from my old apartment-mate, Christine, I am quick to hide it from view. It's a considerably smaller bundle than Bev's, though I'm sure it stretched Christine's budget. With our history of shared food pleasures, I know it's going to be a real treat.

"This bundle is mine, mine, mine, a reward for the demands of life at Sherborne," I sing to myself as I scurry to the upstairs loo, locking the door behind me, and opening the package rapaciously. Two items, both of which Christine and I had savored during our playful time in Chicago—raw cashew butter from Walnut Acres and a box of the renowned Frango chocolate mints from Marshall Field's are inside. Hah! You can't find *those* at Harry's Post Office! I dive in and eat to my heart's content. "Teatime is a little early today," I continue singing, annihilating every morsel that enters my mouth. The lack of such treasures in our diet makes them taste a bit rich. Perhaps that is why I am able to stop eating of my own accord before it's all gone. Sated, I then toddle down the hall to the dorm, and in a generous gesture, offer to share my prize.

As the first third of the course draws to a close before Christmas break, the tension grows. I realize that the feeling of instability is not my own alone. At dinner one night, I sit next to Anna, our ghostly Movements teacher, with Patrick on the other side of me and Sandra, who'd unknowingly broken the little tree, sitting across the table. I am on the verge of tears, hating everything about Sherborne. The cold. Movements. The lectures on our pathetic human condition.

Anna, seeing my state, says to me, "Don't cry now," and begins to tear up herself. Her empathy, which I'd never suspected before, causes me to cry and laugh at the same time.

"I can't even be miserable properly," I tell her.

Something touches my face and when I brush at it, it falls into my hand. A ladybug. In December. I take it to be a good omen.

In practical work for several weeks, I am part of the group whose job is to refinish the stone walls inside the stable block. We are cleaning up the building for human habitation. Wearing facemasks to protect our lungs from the dust, we use wire brushes to take off layers of whitewash and chisels to knock out the old mortar pointing.

The walls, gone over so many times by hand, are almost alive with energy, feeling and looking quite different from stone that's cut by machinery. The stone is shaped—dressed, they call it—by hammer and chisel so they nestle closely against each other, then each stone is stacked in a staggered pattern to create sturdy walls, and mortar is added to make them airtight. These walls had been whitewashed years ago, and now we are cleaning them all to reveal their natural earthy tones and replace loose mortar.

Coincidently, in Theme, we are exploring sensation. By the Friday Theme discussion, despite all the handwork I'm doing, I'm less able to sense than before. Given plenty of opportunity, I manage to remember to sense maybe twice during the entire week. That's a rather small quantity considering how often my hands are hard at work, my negative attitudes alive and kicking, and both could have been reminders to sense myself.

I move through the daily coursework as if in a trance. Only personal conversations with friends and tenderness from Patrick outside of classes cause me to feel any warmth. Yet despite continuing irritability and confusion expressed by so many of us daily, there is no lack of people to describe their positive experiences with the Theme.

How do they manage it? I envy their floating in sensation. They describe how various situations such as gardening to exhaustion, fighting with a group member, or seeing the beauty of the land reminds them to call on their sensation, and when they do, it brings them balance or insight or wisdom. After hearing that, I'm hoping all the more that Mr. B is correct about how, through their work, individuals raise everyone's level of being. Their work seems to be my only hope.

Before the meeting ends, Mr. B lauds Patrick for achieving what we should all be striving toward—'seeing,' not in the visual sense, but in seeing what is needed and then doing it. I guess that's what the fence repair was all about, when he appeared so beatific as he labored out there.

When I lament to Toby my inability to contribute observations to the Theme, he asks, "Haven't you noticed? Every Friday before we meet everyone rushes around after breakfast asking each other what the Theme was this week?"

IF EVERYTHING SEEMS TO BE GOING WELL,
YOU HAVE OBVIOUSLY OVERLOOKED SOMETHING.

Steven Wright

18 ⌘ IN AND OUT OF THE COMFORT ZONE

Because we will not admit our own helplessness, we arrive at a state of tension and conflict in our relations with other people.

JG Bennett

The time has finally come for our groups of thirty-five to be reconfigured. When applying to Sherborne, each of us had filled out a lengthy questionnaire reflecting our interests, covering everything from gardening to music, personality, attitudes, and ways of doing things. We were not told how these forms were going to be used, but the change in groups suggests that they'd been studied in addition to our being observed in our activities.

All of the couples are put together again after being separated during the first configuration. Patrick and I had by chance been in the same group at first. We hadn't come to Sherborne as a couple, so in this new configuration we are kept together. The personality of each new group displays itself in the most distinct way when we do Movements. I feel comfortable being in what I think of as the 'average' group. We are neither exceptionally good nor physically discomfited. I imitate the gestures well and feel them but I can't quite remember what I'm doing. In addition, everyone in our group shares a pleasant lack of assertiveness and moderate competence in contrast to the first group, which is very competitive and includes Bev, and the third, which is somewhat graceless. Or at least that's how I see them at first, but I find the third group's way of moving interesting and wonder what else their unique ways will reveal.

In the new group, I notice Jonas, a good-looking young American who wears saddle shoes, an item of clothing that I always think of as jovial. It must be fifteen years since I last saw a pair. That isn't all about him that makes me chuckle. He often wears a checked sports coat with his jeans and a sage green cotton turtleneck with which he wears a necktie. When I admire his inventiveness, he explains, "It's the only shirt I have with a collar."

Children are allowed to join any activity they have an interest in. Mostly, they're at school during the week, and the younger ones are in Sherborne's day care. Nevertheless, I often see children orbiting around Jonas. Though Mr. B and the staff discourage us from eating outside of meals, I learn that Jonas keeps his pockets full of candy and shares it generously. Also, when he works in the house or garden, he hires all available kids to run errands for him, paying them with change he keeps on hand.

"Get the shovel from the other end of the garden, please," he says. They follow him around like the Pied Piper. He must have discovered the convenience of these arrangements back at home when dealing with his ten younger brothers and sisters.

Around mid-December, another change of activity that accompanies the new group configuration includes studying Turkish with Mr. B. Apparently Turkish is constructed in a manner so different from English that learning it demands thinking in a way that is not automatic for us. Doing anything that requires our attention helps us recognize how often we function without much awareness or while 'being asleep,' as we are so often reminded. Maybe Turkish encourages us to think in the way Hugo had been trying to explain—with less duality than the way English is constructed.

We gather in the downstairs library, our group of thirty-plus not able to fill the room the way the entire student body does during the evening reading. Daylight streams in the windows that are usually shuttered at that time. Before I manage to slide out of view behind one of my classmates, Mr. B nails me with the look and gives me a long sentence to translate. I am completely blank. The most I can do is keep eye contact. I have learned a little vocabulary but don't understand anything about the construction of sentences. The order of the words seems dependent on seeing the universe from the standpoint of an alien life form. Somehow he wills the correct words out of me one by one. I'm not able to remember the sentence long enough to make it upstairs to my journal right after class. All that is left for me to write about is a feeling of great triumph, not in having known the Turkish, but in having continued to look Mr. B in the eye without bursting into tears. Ah well, we all advance at our own level.

Once again, Patrick and I end up spending more time together than intended. While it gives me the intimacy that I hunger for, it also increases the emotional roller coaster. Patrick is quick to 'correct' my attitude whenever I describe feelings at what he considers the wrong time, and then our snapping at each other resumes.

"Apparently you're incapable of understanding what you're supposed to learn from these situations," Patrick says as we face off outside the garden tool shed.

"Why are you so afraid of my having a feeling?" He's more preoccupied with my feelings than I am.

"You're in the wrong center, as usual. This is moving center work," he says pointing to our labor in the garden.

"I can do physical work and still have a feeling about it. Why are you so fearful of feelings?"

"You fool! Why don't you go back to Virginia and your Jesus freaks?"

He's referring to my having been at the Cayce Foundation for the meditation course in the summer preceding Sherborne.

These fights remind me of how confusion in the past led me to wish I could excuse myself from life. I imagine hanging myself. What can I find to do it with? The first thing I see is a roll of toilet paper. Hmm. That won't work. I see myself dropping into the toilet, reaching up to flush and disappearing forever. Maybe I can develop a fatal illness, brain cells wasting away from overuse of the formatory apparatus. But, wait. Isn't freezing supposed to be a painless death? I'll rip off my ski pajamas and fall asleep on *top* of the duvet!

I *am* ruined. I can't even be serious about suicidal depression any more.

IS LIFE WORTH LIVING?
THIS IS A QUESTION FOR AN EMBRYO, NOT FOR A MAN.

Samuel Butler

Other students and even faculty must be feeling a similar confusion when, like cars backfiring, senseless explosions of temper and new affairs are making whispered news in the daily gossip.

In the middle of our silent and serious Morning Exercise, Pierre's wife Vivien stands up and launches into a dramatic rant. The volume of her voice is so shocking I'm unable to take in her exact words. There is a sense of her proclaiming, "How dare you!" as she berates Mr. B, calling his school *foul* and him a hypocrite. In my heart, I am cheering her on and doing etheric back flips. I believe she is a prophetess, speaking for all at this strange school.

On the other end of the scale, amidst the blooming romance category small-framed Toby pairs off with a lovely stout woman whose rosy cheeks are perfect matches for his. The two of them sit close at meal times or tea whispering and then gazing into each other's eyes. They mirror the physically mismatched couples always seen in English comedies, and I wonder if he enacts for her the appropriate Monty Python skits.

The atmosphere of the school is changing again. Sensual high energy pervades it, as we astound ourselves with heroic acts of acceptance, showing love and patience with each other's demands that the garden be dug in such-and-such a manner or the paintbrushes be washed off in just this way. Between blowups, shared laughter brightens the usually dour meetings and classes. One of our classmates, who often plays kitchen diva, shows extraordinary kindheartedness when her assistant burns the vegetables and has to begin the process from scratch.

With the new group configuration, we are told of an additional activity—hosting sporadic visitors' weekends. Prospective students and old students of Mr. Bennett's, dreaming of spiritual refreshment, will arrive on a Friday night for dinner, participate in meditative activities, Movements, and practical work projects during the weekend, and leave after lunch on Sunday.

On the first visitors' weekend, the assertive group is assigned to give the Movements demonstration. They are more than up for it. New white costumes are sewn. Each file of dancers wears different color-of-the-rainbow cumberbunds. The house is buzzing with anticipation, special meals are cooked, and two hundred magnificent peach tarts are prepared for tea.

My group is on house duty. The more tense the atmosphere, the more I wish to retreat to a distant place. I am relieved to be alone cleaning the first floor hallway, far from any activity, dusting the ornate balustrade on the Bennetts' apartment stairway near the cloister and, in the afternoon, cutting and washing countless brussels sprouts the cooks will prepare for dinner. The other potboy and I spend hours with our hands in icy water, focusing on the sprouts that need much cleaning and trimming at the end of the season. The day is at once eternal and instantaneous.

On Sunday afternoon, after the guests leave, we are given an afternoon exeat. Patrick and I decide to walk to Bourton-on-the-Water, about six miles away. The water is what Americans would call a small creek and what the English call the Windrush River. An inn there reminds me of an old fashioned American hotel from my childhood in the 40s. The dining room's large window looks out onto the small hotel terrace and beyond to a velvety lawn that leads right to the edge of the water. We order tea and mixed berries with cream for dessert. I'm enjoying the rare flavors. Patrick is out of sorts again, grumbling and snapping, the reason for it a complete mystery to me. We haven't even been fighting. By the time we get back to school for evening Movements class, I am, for a change, glad to return. We are introduced to a new Movement that soothes me with its prayerful cadence.

Morning Exercise which has been modified weekly, moves from a focus on sensation and breathing to attending to the chakras, using a specific breathing pattern. When Mr. Bennett is asked why we are skipping the heart chakra, he says, "I don't know . . . the heart is best left out for now."

I dreamed yesterday that the ten months were up and I was unable to remember what I'd done or how the course could have gone by so quickly. Today in another dream:

> I am visiting my parents, looking at my old room that has the potential of being bright and cheery. However, I notice that the window still has an awning above it that my parents had installed during my childhood and it is still keeping out the light.

In Movements, sometimes Pierre moves me to the front where I can't copy. By the time I remember the moves I should make, it's too late for my body to respond. Staying in place to continue working is as exhilarating as it is frustrating. Occasionally, I respond body-first, and can see the difference between moving center and head or intellectual center.

When I watch other students during a demonstration, I enjoy seeing the differences among us. Some people convey a compelling presence while others make movements that are unique to them, almost what could be called wrong, but which now reveal something distinctive about the person.

The paradox of Movements is that when you are new to them, they are a powerful challenge to concentration. Once you know them, however, they, instead, activate a prideful attachment, maybe because we work so hard to learn them. Then it's a bigger test to keep the ego from taking control than it is to make an attentive gesture.

Our Theme of 'self-knowledge' seems to be heightening the tense atmosphere. Each day this week my energy is decreasing. Today I am unable to get out of bed until 11:25. I move like a zombie all afternoon until 4:30, when I finally get myself to go to a class. Our group is supposed to work on putting together more Movements costumes. No one remembers what we are supposed to do except me. It doesn't make sense; how is it possible that I am the only one who claims to know what the costumes need? My only wish is to go back to bed but my dorm mate, Renee, takes charge for a moment. "Okay, let's get to work," she orders. Then turning to me, she says, "Show us what to do."

Her confidence in me is energizing. I assign everyone tasks, sorting out what is left of the pile we've been given—some students are to cut fabric from patterns; others are to sew pieces that have already been cut. We work the whole period and it feels great. It's as if I hadn't believed I knew what was needed. How reluctant I am to take any initiative! I need to remember this fluid feeling. No wonder I've been depressed watching myself throughout the week—hell, throughout my life. How often do I miss the opportunity to act against my low expectations of myself? How many of my conclusions are a misinterpretation of what I am capable of doing? Well, it doesn't matter about the past. The question is whether I can make different choices from now on.

Each time I see some weakness in myself, I think maybe I should leave since I can't do the work set out for us. But, failing here, what would I do elsewhere?

> WHETHER YOU BELIEVE YOU CAN
> DO A THING OR NOT, YOU ARE RIGHT.
>
> *Henry Ford*

Patrick and I soften our treatment of each other. We exchange more massages. He teaches me how to sense varying energy in his back, arms, or head and to feel how putting gentle pressure in the air surrounding the physical part evens out the energy. I remember how I used to be able to feel these energies when I was a child. We talk about art and adoringly look over each other's photos.

Patrick invites me to his room after lunch on a day off. We don't discuss what is happening. He takes my hand and leads me to his bed. Without a word, we are hugging and touching each other everywhere. I run my hand over his soft wavy hair and feel his arms wrap around my body. My cheek is against his shaven face. We're sliding beneath the covers while removing each other's and our own clothes so easily I'm not sure how we're managing it. The excitement warms us into activity and exploration. He envelops me and I am enveloping him. I can't believe we've made this unspoken pact of intimacy. I'm so hungry to be near him. When we're satisfied and the room has darkened with the setting of the sun we drift off, awakening just in time for dinner. We manage to get ourselves up, dressing self-consciously. While mumbling see-you-later, we exchange now tentative hugs. Have we done the right thing?

It is almost Christmas and some students are going home. Others are taking a holiday trip. Patrick and I are staying on. We decide I should move into his room, just for Christmas break. We've come to terms with knowing we're not able to keep the peace for long.

He has gotten permission to put together a darkroom in the large coat closet under the apartment staircase. Photography takes on a new dimension. He reminds me how to develop film, which I haven't done since the Art Institute. I love the landscape around Sherborne, aiming my camera at the hills and trees fading into the English fog. In the form of postcards, I mail the photos to my parents with short notes written on the back about what I hope will be activities they can tell their friends and relatives about—what we cook for dinner, the vegetables planted in the garden, where we went on a day off. Mom's response to the pictures is, Doesn't it ever stop raining?

Patrick and I take photos of Pierre's family eagle, falconry being a preoccupation of one of the sons. Playing with the photographic developing reverses some of the darks and lights, giving the pictures an eerie Edgar Allen Poe quality.

Students who stay on during vacation continue to have meals and do a few activities together. The house runs itself without an assignment sheet; everything from washing dishes to caring for the animals is taken care of.

I receive letters from friends—Alan, one of the Jesuit class-mates, Father Robin, and my editorial boss at Who's Who, where I once worked as advertising designer. I'm content with these connections to my old life. I also paint cartoons—about eigh-teen by twenty-four inches. Many of them are playful graphs using sunny side up eggs as markers. Two cartoons have that inspired feeling of having been sent to me from elsewhere. I'm astonished when I look at them. I call the egg graph, *Basic Light Sources,* and the other, a sunnyside up egg hanging on a clothes-line, *Freshly Laundered and Hanging Out to Dry.*

I crochet a sunnyside up egg, build a room screen, and make a coat rack. Doing things I enjoy makes this a real vaca-tion. Mick shows us a prayer Movement, and Pierre shows us another. The slow rocking of the group to chant-like music, arms changing from position to position, rows moving in dif-ferent patterns across the files and back to place is soothing. I love the Movements and their music though I can barely take in any more. From the gentleness of Thanksgiving through the personal and school-bound ups and downs, Christmas break is such a welcome relief that when I think of the immediate future, all I feel is dread for everyone's return.

ANY IDIOT CAN FACE A CRISIS—IT'S THE DAY-TO-DAY LIVING
THAT WEARS YOU OUT.

Anton Chekhov

III

THE MESOTERIC PHASE:

TRANSFORMATION

Christmas Break, 1972 to Spring Break, 1973

19 ❧ THE SEARCH FOR TRANSFORMATION

Respect the act of eating. Reflect on the simple
obvious fact that life has to be given for life.

JG Bennett

It is the last night of vacation, and on my way to the dorm for the night, I meet Zoe in the hall. We don't know each other very well, having never been in the same group, yet there's ease between us. We chat, lamenting about our anxieties over return-ing to the course. She invites me to come with her to Bernice and Dan's room. Sandra is there, too. For the next hour, the five of us commiserate and disparage the enthusiastic students, as if they somehow betray us.

In the morning, I awaken from a nightmare:

> I'm telling Patrick and others about accidentally killing a man a few months before. I worry that, by telling people about it now, I'm in danger of being tracked down by the police. Although I didn't cry at the time we delivered the body to his home, I cry when talking with others about the event, the import of what I've done finally dawning on me.

Am I killing a part of myself by staying here? I value the medita-tive and observational exercises but there is something lacking in the environment . . . empathy? And then there are the sharp tongues of Mr. Bennett's old students. Hardly a day passes without hearing them excuse themselves about raising their voices or being sarcastic and critical. They remind us of the concept that Mr. B mentions often about bearing the unpleasant manifestations of others. They act as if being disagreeable is such a rare fault, they need to intentionally call on it to give us the opportunity to work on ourselves.

No time to give all this more thought. The course starts again now.

SOME PROBLEMS ARE SO COMPLEX THAT YOU HAVE
TO BE HIGHLY INTELLIGENT AND WELL INFORMED JUST
TO BE UNDECIDED ABOUT THEM.

Laurence J. Peter

"Now that Christmas break is over," Mr. B explains, "We are entering a new phase. The purpose of the first three months of the course was to show us our natural state before any process has been applied. All we have done until now is begun to see our nature." He uses an allegory about making bread and compares it to our studies.

"In making bread, as in the course, the first stage reflects the *existence* of the raw materials, the living grains and other ingredients before any process has begun to affect them. Both of these illustrations are examples of what I call the exoteric phase or that which is suitable commonplace knowledge."

"The next stage in making bread," he explains, "is that of harvesting and grinding the grain, mixing it with sugar and yeast, kneading it, allowing it to rise, and baking it—all that goes into transforming the ingredients into bread. This period of transformation is what we are entering now, the mesoteric.'

"The third stage," he says, "is the esoteric, the time of realization. In regard to bread, it means the fulfillment of bread's intended purpose, feeding the community. Some of you will not be able to pass from the exoteric into the mesoteric, and even fewer will go on to fulfill all you can be, but that is the direction of our aim."

At this point, Morning Exercise enters a deeper phase. Mr. Bennett shows us the practice of drawing energy from the sacred geographic locations associated with four great spiritual teachers, Christ, Buddha, Mohammed, and Lama. Energy accumulates in these locations because of people going to them on pilgrimage and praying there. It makes me wonder if the accumulated energy is why we are naturally drawn to places known for their powerful or famous inhabitants?

He has us breathe through the chakras, then send a line from the third eye, pull sacred energy back to ourselves, and blend it by awakening sensation in one limb after another in one of the patterns we've practiced in Movements and Morning Exercise.

I'm not familiar with a couple of the sacred locations but images pop into my mind without thought. I see the desert city, the river crowded with people, the holy cube of a building, and the city built high into the mountains. When photos of them are put up on a bulletin board, I stand before them staring. The visualizations I experienced are much like the pictures.

In the middle of the week, Mr. B decides that we should leave out breathing through the chakras, concentrating more on the sacred locations. During the following week, we continue the same exercise. I must not be the only one having a hard time. He suggests that those who feel blocked should again add in the breathing.

In response to several questions regarding disbelief in what we are doing, he tells us, "Do not pretend to do the exercise. If there is a lack of belief, it is better to take on doing it as a task. That way you can do the important work accomplished by carrying out the exercise, but not by lying or doing it under pretense."

To help us learn something more about ourselves for future Decision work, Mr. B introduces us to the 'Stop!' exercise. The way it functions is that he or someone designated by him will call 'Stop!' several times throughout the day during our activities, loud enough for many of us to hear, even at some distance. Our task is to stop on the physical, emotional, and mental levels and observe what is going on inside ourselves. Some people actually fall over, having stopped their walking at a moment of imbalance.

That shout usually startles me, and by the time I figure out it's the exercise, I'm busy recuperating from feeling angry over having been frightened.

One time I have a fighting chance to participate because I'm off on the periphery of being able to hear the shout at all. Val and I are servers returned to the servery to pick up more bowls of soup to carry to people seated at the dining tables. She and I both reach out to grasp the same bowl with our right hands when Mr. B, at the far end of the dining hall, calls 'Stop!' I see how the cook, Val, and I are physically linked to one another. I had just set eyes on Val, gazing in admiration of her geisha-like beauty—black shiny hair pulled back, an image of serenity and purpose. Another time I'm not jolted into frightened anger, what I see is that I'm nowhere inside myself, not observing anything until we stop.

Yet, another 'Stop!' catches me mid-sentence and although I discontinue speaking and gesturing with my hand, there is energy accompanying my actions that simply continues to flow away—whoooooooossssh! Like a balloon that had been blown up and then released.

In this mesoteric stage of study and a week after initiating the 'Stop!' practice, Mr. B thinks we are ready to move ahead with the Decision Exercise. He wants us to use it to modify a personal characteristic rather than to carry out a physical activity. The Decision should take us two weeks to complete.

"Two weeks," he says, "is enough time to prepare you to change a negative characteristic or habit." Many students choose to work on their smoking or eating addictions.

One of the principles of the Decision Exercise is to design it always using a positive action. After all, if we could just stop doing whatever bad habit we have by saying to ourselves, "I won't do that anymore," we would. Instead, the idea is to draw on the urge or energy of the habit as a positive reminder by blending it within ourselves, as we've practiced in Morning Exercise and Movements.

Mr. B gives an example of how to work on giving up smoking. "Notice when you have the urge to smoke. Use it to remind yourself of your decision. Rather than fighting the desire, do something positive with the impulse. Blend 'I have the urge to light up a cigarette' with sensing 'I am' in your chest or with breathing the urge into your feeling center."

I decide to chip away at the habit I have of intending to be humorous by making self-deprecating remarks aloud, such as saying it's only my body that's reluctant to sweep again, my mind finds it thought-provoking. I notice that these remarks set me up to be treated in a way I later resent, like when someone purposely assigns me to do something they think I dislike because they have decided it's good for me.

Every day for two weeks I do the same exercise. I stop myself from speaking the thoughts aloud and blend the urge into my heart while attending to my breath. Doing the exact same exercise each day changes my awareness and tempers my automatic behavior. However, when we meet to discuss the exercise I get the idea that we were supposed to have experimented with different ways of working toward our goal. Without asking to clarify my understanding, I take solace in my possible mistake when Mr. Bennett reminds us once again that, "No effort is ever lost." Rarely do I ask questions. I still think, as in my childhood, that I am supposed to figure things out by listening and watching and not making trouble for anyone else.

Discussions about this exercise tend to become very complex. Some cases cry out for legal advice. For example, Vinnie says, "I gave up dessert and then we were given apples for dessert. But apples are healthy. I never consider them dessert. In my mind, I gave up naughty desserts. So my question is: Is it legal for me to eat one? Am I sworn to abide by the word 'dessert' when my intentions focused on the concept of health?"

The plethora of subtle opinions would have impressed a court of law. As a group, we conclude after careful interrogation that Vinnie is bound to the word 'dessert' until setting a new exercise because he visualized the offending food as that which is called dessert and served after dinner. In a new exercise, he can specify sugar or whatever it is he considers unhealthy.

GUILT: THE GIFT THAT KEEPS ON GIVING

Emma Bombeck

We still often return to the issue of likes and dislikes. By this point in the year, I've done every task so often that I've had numerous good and bad moments with them all. Do I like doing dishes? It's easy; the water is warm; having clean dishes pleases me. Do I dislike doing the dishes? My hands get so wrinkled and dry it requires constant use of lotion to keep them soft; if I'm not vigilant enough, they crack and bleed; the water gets greasy and disgusting; washing dishes can be mind numbing.

Instead of feeling free of likes and dislikes, I'm trapped in hesitation, not knowing my opinions anymore. I see how any feeling easily becomes its opposite. And I also see that in many situations, whether I like or dislike something just isn't relevant.

This morning, the building is so silent I could be convinced it's been abandoned. Once again I'm sweeping the endless upstairs hall. When I get as far as whisking out the alcove to men's dorm #10, from the direction of the dining hall, I hear the sound of running footsteps. I stand there curious, resting on my broom and waiting for the person to make an appearance from around the corner, perhaps thirty feet away.

Pierre explodes into view and, after a couple of enthusiastic leaps, much to my amazement, goes flying through the air, landing horizontally on the floor with a small thump. I've seen this happen often enough that I no longer start running to him. As if knowing I'm staring at him from down the hall, he lifts his head and gazes directly into my eyes with unsmiling indifference. In a blink, he shifts to verticality, seamlessly reentering his running path. I ask my friends about this phenomenon. No one else has ever seen him trip, slip, or fall as I have. Is the Universe sending me a message, poor Pierre its messenger?

FALL DOWN SEVEN, GET UP EIGHT.

Japanese Proverb

The pattern of our weeks continues on, Mr. B usually introducing a new Theme every Monday and overseeing our observations every Friday. The subject matter of Themes has been wide ranging, covering everything from the most concrete, such as 'material objects' or 'food,' to issues that could be called ethereal, such as 'energies' or 'listening'. However, even the most tangible Theme turns out to inspire observations about intangibles: awareness, effort, relationship, accountability, and gratitude. This time we are to ask ourselves: For what stakes are we playing this game? Why are we here?

"You must understand the difference between thinking about the question and understanding that the question is there." It is all I can do to repeat his statement to myself.

While he is making his introduction, I believe that my soul is at stake—that that's why I'm here. However, the inability to carry out or sometimes even understand our assignments continues to feel devastating. In the back of my mind, I'm always wondering if I shouldn't leave. Then I think, isn't there still a glimmer of hope that remaining at Sherborne will help me find a clearer sense of purpose?

Occasionally a Theme impresses itself on my awareness with such intensity that even though I make no observations of my own nor remember anyone else's, at least Mr. B's introduction stays with me. He is talking about life and its relationship to food, his glance moving from student to student.

"I want you to take note of what happens when you come into contact with food." He folds his hands and closes his eyes as if following his own suggestion. I think he must be talking about greed, hunger, comfort, gusto, and those sorts of ideas. Also, I remember how we arrived at Sherborne in time for harvest and how only with experience in the garden and kitchen am I learning what is involved in growing and preparing food, how contact with the soil is making me aware of our dependence on the earth.

He look at us again and asks, "Do you appreciate that, when we eat, another life form gives up its existence for us? We cannot survive eating dirt and air. It takes life to give us life. Do you also understand that every form of life has qualities that we cannot provide for ourselves?"

I can contemplate such ideas once he says them, but I'd never think about food in those terms on my own. My choice of a vegetarian diet that was offered to us, for example, comes

from challenges with my health, not from concepts about killing animals.

He asks, "Does our having available to us a variety of food
mean we also have available different types of behavior? Is this
not true about climate and the kinds of foods that grow in them?
Does not the eating of meat and grains make us take for granted
the killing of life forms in a way that is different from those who
eat fruit and eggs and cheese where the plant or animal does not
die but only shares its produce?

"Likewise, the more food is packaged and processed, the
more distant we are from its living form. We no longer even
know where the food comes from," he says. "Keeping my questions in mind will help you make observations about our contact with food.

"I want you to look beyond egoistic needs for particular diets, vitamin supplements, and other notions about good
and bad food. Such attitudes focus our attention on ourselves
instead of on the gift we've been given.

"We are not talking about eating from a physical or even
a psychological point of view. I want you to discover what it
would mean to eat in a right way in a spiritual sense. With the
right inner state we can transform any kind and very little food
from the physical into the spiritual. By consciously eating, we
can fulfill food's destiny while working toward fulfilling our
own. Have you not heard of the Indian saints who survive for
years eating only an orange a day? All food can be nourishing if
you have the right inner state."

What Mr. B says gives me a different way to look at all the
conflicting ideas I've read about for years regarding diet. How
will I reconcile his thoughts with my own health issues?

20 ∾ HITS OF ENERGY

Until we try, we cannot tell what we can do.

JG Bennett

It is January 13. Sherborne is holding an open house to celebrate Mr. Gurdjieff's birthday. Students will give a Movements demonstration and prepare a feast. There's also going to be a ritual that staff and students are excited about—the toast to the idiots, which was one of Gurjieff's methods for teaching about the hazards of humans trying to become their true selves. The toasting ceremony includes drinking hard liquor. I was intending to avoid the toasts because of the intensity of the atmosphere and not wanting to drink.

For the last week, I've not been feeling well, and in the last three days my head has been pulsating with waves of pain. Yesterday, the rock musician Arthur Brown visited, playing electronic music at a volume that I survived only by seeking the far corners of the house. In the evening I learned I'm appointed house supervisor for today's celebration. With one hundred and three people on the course, it is inevitable that I would get the assignment soon. So much for planning on not being here.

It's a big deal for me. I never would have volunteered for the job, especially on a day that is considered critical. In my family, we learned that big responsibilities are impossible to handle. My brother and I were never assisted in learning how to do something we thought might be difficult. What sustains me is that it is a silent day. Yes, I find that advantageous!

Dozens of volunteers show up all day long, silently saluting me, conveying their willingness to accept assignments for house duty. Some are from the two groups of students not on house duty and others are guests, everyone working as hard as the people in our group. It never would've occurred to me to volunteer to do housework for another group, although it reminds me how as a child I wanted to try everything I saw other people doing. Then, it was all play. When had that changed? When had activity become such a burden? Could I change it back to how it once was?

Someone lets me know with a written note that Ivo had stopped by this morning and asked about me. He must have thought he would have been interrupting to seek me out in the midst of my obligations. I'm agitated to learn I've missed him.

I'm still working on the Decision Exercise of not making negative statements about myself aloud. Since it is a silent day and since I'm not supposed to speak, my negative thoughts do not linger as long as usual. Also, my co-workers are spared any inclination I might have to make helpful suggestions.

It amazes me again how the dining hall can be transformed into a glittering interior of some medieval castle. Candles flickering and sumptuous decorations are called up from nothing. Platters overflow with food, and Mr. B leads mysterious toasts that refer to the idiotic qualities of different human types. I lack the expectancy and anticipation the other students have for this ritual. Nevertheless, as I fall into bed exhausted and not the usual wound-up, I'm satisfied that the day went well.

Only two days later we have another silent day. Instead of the reading before dinner, we are assigned to sit in silence for forty-five

minutes recalling each hour of the day. My meditation is chaotic, jumping from one thought to another. Am I fulfilling the
assignment? I think back on the waves of love I felt coming from
geisha-like Val when we were working together. Images of the
day are sprinkled with scenes of childhood—hoping for a hop-
scotch partner, roller derby with my brother on the cement base-
ment floor, making "salad" with the backyard plants by myself.
This was a distant past before I'd learned how to make pleasant
conversation or humorous gibes to attract laughter and approval.
Those youthful moments were simple but heavy with isolation, a
different kind of complexity than now.

Often, during the day today I thought I might burst into
tears. Yet to allow the draining of emotion might have stolen
away too much energy. An image comes of solemn Jim when we
worked out in the garden. Spattered with mud from head to toe,
Jim's wellies were caked, his plaid flannel shirt askew, one tail of
it hung out from the side of his bib overalls as he grinned at me
impishly, also sending unexpected waves of warmth.

Several times during the exercise, when I achieve some
quiet inside, I fall asleep, my head jerking suddenly as my chin
hits my chest. For the last fifteen minutes of this reading time we
practice the Zikr, an Islamic meditation that Mr. B introduced
us to last week. The method requires a breathing pattern of one
inhalation and three exhalations. At intervals, he knocks on the
floor as a signal to hold our breaths. With a second knock, we
return to the patterned breathing.

Mr. B tells us, "Breathing occupies you so that you will interfere as little as possible with what is accomplished on another
level." Accomplished by whom? Level of what? I never ask, but

Jenny, the girl who has no self-consciousness, does. I can't remember his exact words, perhaps intimations of higher consciousness being able to do its job because the rhythmic breathing elevates us to a place beyond the material world, disconnecting us from our habitual thoughts.

It is Monday morning and at Morning Exercise, Mr. B sits on a cushion at the far end of the ballroom. Though we can barely see him in the darkness of the winter morning, we know he is wearing as usual his hound's tooth jacket with the leather elbow patches. He introduces what he calls the sacred impulses— Wish, Hope, Belief, Will, and Love. He explains that man's ordinary being is dualistic. We tend to pit one thing against another. Good and bad. Stupid or intelligent. Light or dark.

"This exercise will be especially useful for us who live in Western culture. Eastern religions," he explains, "have a detailed understanding of the holy architecture of the body and how to access it to enhance spiritual life. One of those structures, known as the five sacred impulses, are also called the five positive emotions or latifas. They appear to have physical locations in the body, but actually they are points of contact between the physical body and the different energy bodies that all people possess. Unlike so much of what we human beings perceive, the sacred impulses are not dualistic. They don't have a good aspect and a bad aspect. They are simply stronger or weaker and can be strengthened through meditative exercise."

Mr. Bennett tells us, "We often spoil the impulses by interpreting them in the wrong way. We *Wish* to have something, *Hope* for results, *Believe* in creeds or people, use *Will* to do our own bidding, and *Love* with an agenda." I could almost grasp his uncommon explanation by thinking of them as cosmic qualities that stand on their own rather than as action verbs that carry an object.

"We must look at these real emotions in a different way," Mr. Bennett says, "understanding that they are already inside ourselves. They are our Oneness with Spirit, quite unlike our painful looking to something outside ourselves."

Our group is preparing to do the Movements demonstration for the next visitors' weekend. Anna, our most frequent teacher at this time, often moves me to the back row, but today, she moves me to the front. It feels like a conspiracy after just having been house supervisor for Gurdjieff's birthday, but as happens more often lately, I become energized by the extra effort that being in the front row requires. My work is not so much in doing the Movements correctly, as much as it is in keeping my cool despite my inevitable mistakes. I just continue or start again without displays of confusion or apology.

Pierre, too, is putting attention on me, this time out in the garden, as in the beginning of the course, asking me if the work I'm doing is what I had been assigned. My reactions are much the same internal grumbling about him but also don't cause the lengthy spill into inner considering. They just are what they are.

The next day at breakfast, a list of names, including mine, is read aloud. We are told to pick up a written message. I don't know if the others receive the same one, but mine says I am to dress in my gardening clothes before Morning Exercise from now on. Changing clothes after breakfast is causing me to arrive late for practical work.

I hate waiting, even a minute, so after weeks of arriving on time and having to wait for latecomers to show up, I, too, drift into turning up late. Since I'm capable of being on time, my failure to do so is embarrassing and angering. At the same time, accepting my own reactions and deciding to attend to the note gives me another little hit of energy.

Mr. B's presence continues to fill whatever room he is in. A direct look from him still sets me quaking with fear or energy. Sometimes he acts intent on directing toward me a thought or an ability to act. Whatever his intention, I resent my awe as much as my terror. It's too unbalanced. Maybe that's why I note the fog so often in my journal or photographs. It cushions the hard edges.

A small group of women learned a women's mourning Movement that is very different from the more gentle 'Assyrian Women Mourners' that we learned earlier in the course. The rest of us women are invited into the ballroom. We sit on the floor watching them. It is a dramatic dance, each woman whirling, spinning in despair, rotating the head to make her hair fly in all directions, moving to the haunting music. After some minutes, Mr. B conveys that we may join in whenever we feel ready.

I am divided, curious to see what it feels like, wanting to please Mr. B, but too shy to perform so theatrical a dance. Mr. B must sense my indecision. Impatient with my reticence, perhaps hoping to move me beyond indecision and into what he knows I can do, he walks toward where I sit. I shudder and refuse to look at him as he stops in front of me, and I sense his height like being in the shadow of a skyscraper. His hands grasp my shoulders, and he easily lifts me up to stand me on my feet. Staring into his chest and feeling violated by his *help*, I sink back down to the floor, and he lets me be. I'm just not ready.

YIELD TO TEMPTATION.
IT MAY NOT PASS YOUR WAY AGAIN.

Lazarus Long

Our group holds one of those free form classes where we can ask questions of Mr. B. He speaks about the strain in the atmosphere. I am glad to hear my classmates volunteer their opinions when I don't have the nerve to say anything myself. They bring up lack of community, how we don't display responsibility for each other, and the absence of family feeling.

Mr. B asks, "Is it good to have family feeling? Why?"

He lets us think about it for a couple of minutes. Then he speaks again.

"It is important for you to see how we have not developed real relationships. Most of what we think of as relationships is just personality with no essence or commitment behind it."

After that class we discuss among ourselves about what Mr. Bennett's words might mean in terms of how we behave with each other. It's easy to be lackadaisical about relationship at Sherborne. We're together every day in our limited environment. What would it take to transform our predictable interactions into caring bonds?

A visitor from the first year course comes to Sherborne for a few weeks. Axel, with his sandy blond shoulder length hair feels like an old friend. Our paths first cross in the garden where we conversed with each other. He was born with one arm a good deal shorter than the other, and while he was on the first year course, he fell off a ladder and broke the full length arm. This caused all sorts of inconveniences, not only for him but for those who had to help him get dressed and undressed and use the bathroom. He tells me about these adventures with good-humored energy.

"Tell me another story," I say to Axel one afternoon during a teatime stroll in the garden before he'd seen any of my artwork.

Without hesitation, he says, "Have you heard about the Zen master who told his student to guess what he had in his pocket?"

"No," I say. So Axel tells it to me:

"It's shaped like an egg, yellow and white inside and hard outside," said the teacher.

The student asked, "Is it a rock?"

"No."

"Is it a small covered bowl filled with rice and squash?"

"No."

"Is it a cake with hard icing?"

"No, none of those things."

"Well, what is it?" asked the student.

"An egg," said the master.

I invite Axel up to the dorm and show him the egg cartoons I made at Christmas. We laugh over the fitting story he'd chosen to tell me.

Maybe it was the easy rapport with Axel that inspired me to show Russ, the art teacher, some sketches from my previous summer's journal. The stiff symmetrical symbols are from a numinous dream I'd had. They are pyramids seen from above, two squares with lines indicating that each corner of the square leads to the apex. One square glows light and the other radiates flames. I had awakened from these images filled me with eager expectation.

"Your drawings are pretty superficial," Russ says.

I don't express the inner 'ouch' I'm feeling. What's there to say? Here I am exposing a mood of hope that had finally begun burning within me, and he saw nothing in them.

I WAS GOING TO BUY A COPY OF *THE POWER OF POSITIVE THINKING*, AND THEN I THOUGHT: WHAT THE HELL GOOD WOULD THAT DO?

Ronnie Shakes

After lunch I'm still annoyed with Russ. Needing to escape the tearoom clamor, I go to the copse where we had cut up the storm-felled ash tree. Nearby stands a rectangular garden gazebo—a folly the English called it—about ten by twenty feet, perhaps eight feet high, shaped like a Greek temple with fluted columns and a bench under its roof. Instead of facing into the dark woods of our property, the bench looks in the opposite direction, maybe thirty feet from the fence line, toward the neighbor's bright open meadow with cows grazing far in the distance.

No one comes out here much; at least, I never bump into anyone. I enjoy the grand architectural expression in what feels like humble human scale. Sitting on the bench after a few deep sighs of self-pity, I close my eyes to meditate. I'm not sure how long I sit; it can't be more than fifteen minutes. When I open my eyes, staring back at me are twenty pairs of soulful cows' eyes. All the pale brown jerseys from the field have lined themselves up, quiet as mice, in neat order at the fence to attend to me.

From that time on, whenever I visit, I stay long enough to say hello to them. Had my eyes been open the first time it happened, I'd have learned that all it takes is one cow becoming aware of my presence to initiate a silent gathering from all corners of the field.

21 ❧ JONAS

My place is where I am, and your place is where you are. Not only have I got to bear my own situation, I have to bear your situation also. First of all I have to bear the truth about myself and little by little I have to bear all truths.

JG Bennett

One of the phrases of the Work lexicon is "work on oneself." It refers to the efforts we make to develop our consciousness. I hear it used most often by Work veterans when someone is disagreeing with them.

"But I already weeded that plot in the garden."

"Oh, go Work on yourself."

Or someone is talking about an event in her life, saying, "It breaks my heart that we had a fight." And even a sympathetic respondent might reply, "Jeez, *you* need to Work on yourself." Does something about the Work stop people from listening to someone's point of view or asking a person what they think they need to make a situation better? The week after having set us a Theme to examine 'Work on oneself,' Mr. B speaks with us about it, again.

"We cannot begin work on ourselves until we learn we are ordinary. All of what we think of as our internal differences is irrelevant. What is important is that we are people. That is what we have in common—the seed of an immortal soul."

Morgan speaks in class about viewing himself as empty. It requires more faith than he has to believe in an 'I.' To him, 'Work on oneself' is work on what isn't there in order to find what is. His phrase makes an odd kind of sense to me. You work to come up with better understanding or a better solution than your original unsatisfactory response to something. The effort shows you what is missing or what you can do when you try.

Then Morgan tells a story of how during Morning Exercise, he didn't see his wife Betty sitting across the room in her usual spot. He couldn't get his mind away from worrying about her. This occupied him during half the Morning Exercise. After twenty minutes or so, there she was! He realized she must have been there all along.

Mr. B says, "The illusion is no less formidable because of its being an illusion."

Following the strain in the air after Christmas break, everyone acts as if they are high, once again cheery and helpful. It's so delightful that I give it no thought. Patrick says he wants more time alone, and I'm glad to have both more time to myself and more time to be with other people. I take up studying Turkish after lunch with several members of our current group. Yet while I enjoy the amiable talking and laughter, I can't help worrying that I might come crashing down from these ebullient days.

It is Saturday open house again, and due to our good moods, it feels like a party for the first time—everyone quick to laugh and applaud, none of the usual Work somberness. I feel no need to escape the weekend crowd. Late at night, when the festivities are over, I have so much energy I decide to go do my laundry. After that's finished, still unable to consider sleeping, I walk down to the Great Hall. I find Teresa there looking like a medieval princess, her red hair flowing past her shoulders, a scoop neck midnight blue dress frames her pale face and neck. She sings and plays her guitar by the fireplace. Without stopping, she conveys an invitation to join her, which I do for about half an hour until she excuses herself to go to bed; I stay on, singing to myself.

Not long afterward, Jonas of the cheery saddle shoes shows up and hints that he's been noticing me. In some meandering way, we broach the unforeseen subject of my mother's recent letter. Something, perhaps the foggy post cards, has reminded her of the misfortune of my ten-year–old-self losing an umbrella.

"But what are we discussing?" I ask Jonas. "What is my umbrella doing here now?"

"Everybody's welcome," Jonas says, "even your umbrella."

At tea one day, Patrick approaches me.

"I want to tell you where I'm at," he says.

I expect this is going to be unpleasant, yet, we need the communication. He brings up our being dependent and possessive with each other. I don't disagree. And, by the way, he adds, "I'm not finished with Janie at Beshara, and I realize it's made me feel unable to commit to you." My relief surprises me at first, but it confirms something I sensed and couldn't put my finger on.

The warm friendly atmosphere of the school, following the rampant dissatisfaction of a couple of weeks before, continues for another few days. Although I no longer think the change of moods in the environment are personal anymore, I still want to attribute them to something. Maybe the new meditations help or maybe the increased sunlight as winter passes. Perhaps we have grown more comfortable with the demands of school and each other. Could these fluctuations of disposition have a natural rhythm that in the greater world goes unnoticed amidst the complications of modern life?

Any sadness I feel about Patrick is countered by the general mood of good will and playful banter of Toby, Gertie, Lucas, Betty, and Vinnie, who has come to bill himself as 'the kissing bandit' and always sends air kisses my way when we pass in the halls. I also have the pleasure of my continuing preoccupation with giving haircuts.

Marcella is chief cook and mother hen this afternoon when I am on kitchen duty. She shoos me out of the room between tea and dinner to take a break. That's never happened before. I say to myself, 'If I go to the Great Hall, I'll meet Jonas.' As soon as I turn the corner, there he is coming toward me. The following afternoon we come upon each other again and, this time, we skip the reading and dinner to take a long walk.

THE TROUBLE WITH REAL LIFE IS
THAT THERE'S NO DANGER MUSIC.

Jim Carrey

The Turkish study group meets today in men's dorm room 10. Dallas, one of the roommates along with Toby and Lucas, greets me, radiating his Southern warmth. I look around the room I'd been in only once during the apple cider party. One of the upper bunks is filled with clutter. "No one sleeps *there*, do they?" I ask.

"That's Jonas's bed!"

"Does he sleep with all that stuff there?"

"Yep," Dallas says, and with what I could swear is pride, adds, "and even when he changes the sheets, he leaves it all there."

"He must be a genius," I mutter while conjuring up a picture of him in my mind. His personal grooming never hints of anything like this. From where I'm standing, I can see a heap of books, papers, a bag of candy, a sandwich, bottles, and blankets. Pinned on the wall are letters, old wrappers, advertisements, and photographs. Later in the day, when I return to my dorm between classes, Jonas shows up grinning. He hands me figs and cookies. How sweet! I stand there beaming back at him.

As Patrick and I see each other less, Jonas and I spend more time together, taking long walks or hanging out in his dorm after lunch. He always wears the jaunty saddle shoes, a feather in his lapel, and a leaf stuck by the stem into his navy knit cap. He's a troubadour who doesn't sing, the fool in a Tarot deck promising new beginnings.

A favorite pastime of Jonas's is to open a book at random and read to me or have me read to him. At first, this method shocks my sensibilities—so chaotic, so anarchistic! How can there be order in a universe where one enters a story in the middle? But then, I think back to the first time Mick showed me the garden and made me realize we were harvesting the bounty of the first year students' labors. I am reminded again how life is exactly like that. Everywhere we go and in everything we do, we enter in the middle . . . and leave in the middle, too. We always build on the work done before we came along and how often we wish to leave behind something worthwhile for future generations, at the very least for our own progeny. I soon attune to the poetry of Jonas's inclinations and relish them.

I peek into the kitchen window from the courtyard and see Jonas cutting onions and smiling to himself. I decide to go in and tell him I saw him smile. Before I get a word out, he says, "I was thinking of you."

While I'm standing there chatting with him, Ginny, one of Betty and Morgan's daughters comes in and asks Jonas, "Where's my father?"

Jonas lifts one lid after another, staring into each kettle and chanting in a singsong tone, "He isn't in *here* . . . he isn't in this one . . . I don't know where he's gone." Ginny smirks and gives Jonas a slap on the behind for being so silly.

We're in Jonas's dorm at lunchtime on a weekend day when some of the older kids burst into the room. They want paid work and, as usual, he has something for them to do, never short of ideas or change to pay them with. This time he sends them to help the a.m. service crew clean up lunch. The crew must think the children are setting up a diabolical scheme to destroy the dining hall.

> HELL, THERE ARE NO RULES HERE—
> WE'RE TRYING TO ACCOMPLISH SOMETHING.
>
> *Thomas A. Edison*

The first time Jonas and I go on exeat together, a welcome day off, it is to Oxford, about thirty miles away. On the way to the bus stop, Jonas offers me a peanut butter and jelly sandwich he's saved from lunch a couple of days ago.

"No thanks," I decline, though admiring his forethought.

As we walk along the back road and then to the big highway where we are going to catch the bus, we notice the large trucks the English called lorries. I point out how in America, the broad ones are labeled 'Wide Load' across the rear bumper. In England they are labeled 'Oversize Vehicle,' plenty of room for all those letters and so much more British sounding.

We wander Oxford's campus, admiring the quadrangles, the venerated architecture, and the Ashmolean Museum of Art and Archaeology. We also explore the center of town and drift for hours in Blackwell's book and art shop, the size of a small country. After this intimate time with each other, we cut out of several readings the following week, choosing to use the time for meditation, prayer, and snuggling.

The next time Jonas and I go on exeat, he carries a bulky rucksack. As we amble down the country lanes, he reveals the contents, one item at a time. "I made us some sandwiches," he says and also produces bright colored bags of pretzels and other snacks picked up at the Post Office. At intervals, he pulls out a half dozen different books from which we read as the day progresses.

As we walk, he picks up different objects and stuffs them into his bag. Some are appealing natural items—a leaf or a rock—and some manmade, ordinary refuse. At first, I think he is keeping the environment clean and intending to throw it away, but he waves me away when I point to a trashcan in front of a cottage.

Instead, once back at Sherborne, I watch as he inserts every piece into his personal space. A desiccated rose is used to decorate his hat, a discarded flyer becomes a bookmark; a sheet of paper litter with directions someone had scrawled on one side becomes the backside of a letter Jonas writes to a friend. The interesting tidbit on the back suggesting a trip made is never mentioned in Jonas' letter.

Now I understand his dorm area, the upper bunk where he sleeps is filled with flotsam and jetsam. At the ends of the bed, he has created walls with several tall metal lockers on one end and two stacked chests of drawers at the other. His dorm mates refer to his bunk as 'the nest.' All of the items that called out to him are taped on the wall alongside the length of the bed and the half-walls created by the lockers and chests. His careful placement of them in relation to each other gives them additional meanings they had not possessed before his receptivity touched them.

We often sequester ourselves in the nest for short periods after lunch or tea to cuddle, his kind roommates ignoring us. Each day I look forward to seeing what bits of glittery trash the crow might have added, hoping to discover something I haven't seen before, some ancient ad from a magazine juxtaposes images of feet and shoes, a smiling housewife displaying a glowing cleaning product seems to illustrate a poem by Emily Dickenson.

I compare myself to Jonas. While I make lengthy lists, write notes in my journal, find it trying to do whatever I've committed to, Jonas floats through life like a dandelion seed buffeted about in a windy sky, seeming to have no need for ordinary organization. Does he remember everything he wants to do? Does he have things he wants to remember? He *has* memorized all sixty-four hexagrams of the I Ching, the Chinese book on divining. Why and how has he done that?

In Theme, Mr. Bennett introduces the concept of the third line of work. He compares it to the first line where we go from being asleep to awakening, perfecting ourselves as far as possible. In the second line, we move from being awake to becoming active, helping others. In the third line, we are manifesting the active force, fulfilling the true purpose of human existence. As much as I hunger for purpose, I can't yet imagine just how this third line will look.

The lectures are permeated with vocabulary that Mr. B developed from his studies of science and philosophy with Gurdjieff, Ouspensky, and other spiritual teachers. His presentations are so clear and methodical that I sometimes grasp what he is saying, but the feeling of crushing responsibility simultaneously pushes me away. The words chide us for being asleep, being mechanical, not working hard enough, and being unable to *do* anything. No efforts are ever sufficient. It mimics the language of high expectations that I grew up with. Although the intent was admirable, the standards could never be met and an attendant lack of nurturing then and now seems to be the norm.

Unlike Sherborne's aims, however, the destination of my parent's world was to live a common existence, a comfortable material reality. With Gurdjieff, the sense of aim is pervasive. We are, at the very least, to live honorably, at the most, to assist the Great Creator in maintaining the universe. This will be accomplished by being aware of one's obligation to pay for one's existence, never giving up, no matter what we believe to be in store for us beyond death.

How many of us came to Sherborne hoping for a new start in life? But it is not so easy, for in reality we came here in the middle of our own stories. And, for me, as much as I value this school experiment, for the sake of my mental health, I also need to resist the attending spirit in which the lessons are expressed. Jonas helps me do that with his abundant tenderness and humor.

22 ∾ THERE'S ALWAYS ROOM FOR CONFLICT

O, y the interaction of conflicting processes can break the vicious circle of repeating what is no longer serving any purpose.

JG Bennett

Patrick, watching Jonas and me spend time together, comes up to me this morning. With a sneer, he says, "Has Jonas caught the disease I once had? It can't be cured, you know."

Patrick's ill will darkens my mood again; meditation and Zikr doesn't lift it. Hoping to divine an attitude adjustment from the sixty-four hexagrams of the I Ching, I toss the three coins. Each of six tosses indicates an arrangement of heads and tails. Then I look up that specific pattern in the book. It comes to number 36, Darkening of the Light. I make notes in my journal quoted from the book. The "he" being referred to is the coin tosser, me.

"The name of the hexagram means literally 'wounding of the bright'; hence the individual lines contain frequent references to wounding . . . . One must not unresistingly let himself be swept along by unfavorable circumstances, nor permit his steadfastness to be shaken . . . . One should let many things pass without being duped."

Here I am, driven to applying omens to my own circumstances, looking for consolation from a book of divination. Well, I got some and there was more.

"If he does not want to make compromises within himself, but insists on remaining true to his principles, he suffers deprivation. Nevertheless he has a fixed goal to strive for, even though the people with whom he lives do not understand him and speak ill of him . . . . In order to escape danger, they need invincible perseverance of spirit and redoubled caution in their dealings with the world . . . . Here the climax of the darkening is reached . . . . in the end it perishes of its own darkness . . . ."

That'll show 'em, and I keep going another day.

A few weeks later Patrick seeks me out again, this time to say he is writing a poem about me in his head inspired by a photograph he took of me walking down the road. It made him feel nostalgic

and brought up images of Charlie Chaplin, the famous come-
dian from silent films and a favorite of mine, whose character of
a guileless soul is shown at the end of each film traveling down
the road and kicking up his heels on the way to his next adven-
ture. Patrick also says, "I see Jonas in a different light, especially
after seeing your painting of a winged saddle shoe." The shoe is
flying in a blue sky accompanied by fluffy white clouds.

At this point in the year, Mr. Bennett, perhaps inspired by the
number of questions people had when they sought his coun-
sel or perhaps because of what he observes among his students,
announces that he will give a lecture about sex. It causes quite
a stir of anticipation. Most members of our generation haven't
ever heard someone from his generation speak on the topic.

"Ideal sex would take place when each partner has no feelings toward the other," he explains. "Sex becomes evil when it
is connected with the other centers—when it is emotional, possessive, or affects the ability to think."

Being a mere mortal, I'm not sure I can even imagine what
he is talking about. I'm glad to be young enough to think there
is plenty of time to discover the meaning of what he is saying.
Maybe some day his lectures, which are being recorded, will be
available for further study.

Mr. B describes three kinds of sex: pure animal, procre-
ational, and supernatural. He says. "Sex is a very high state of
energy. A marriage with true union can provide the environment for the birth of a superior being."

"The man and woman can be two bodies, have two feelings, yet be one in essence. Love cannot exist where there is

possessiveness or jealousy." All I can think of is how all my sad and conflicted friends and I grew up in environments that were anything but unified.

He explains that sex has a very important function relating to the regulation of both creative and tainted energies. "Sex can provide harmonization and elimination of energies where it is needed. For example, sexual energy can support creativity by stilling the mind and at the same time keeping it alert to that which is new and given to us from outside."

He also points out that in the evolutionary scheme of things, with sex comes birth and death. The self-creating amoeba or algae are identical, immortal, not knowing birth or death. In another lecture on the topic, Mr. B says, "In the world of sperm, conceptions are as rare as a perfected being is in the world of men."

LIFE IS A SEXUALLY TRANSMITTED DISEASE.

R.D. Laing

Each of Mr. B's comments piques my interest enough to store them in some internal safe-deposit box but not enough to try to understand them in the moment. They require more attention than I have available. Meanwhile I spend more time with Jonas whose goofy humor and unpredictable views on life keep me engaged in ways I more easily recognize.

Despite Jonas's and my mutual appreciation of meditation and prayer and my admiration for his flowing interactions with people, I still feel uneasy when I see him in pleasant conversation with my roommate Amber. The irony of my strong judgment about thinking he's attracted to a woman who is needy and deluded doesn't escape me. However, this morning during a complex meditative exercise combining the sacred emotions and Zikr, for a split second, I enter the personage of an Indian saint and feel love for Amber. In that instant, I cherish her and see her as a complete and tender human being, suffering, struggling, and trying to thrive. If only I could be this way all the time.

THAT LOVE THY NEIGHBOR THING - I REALLY MEAN IT.

God

Dallas loans Jonas a book that he misplaces. Pierre finds it and returns it to Dallas whose name is in it. When Dallas asks Pierre where it had been, Pierre refuses to tell, saying that he should know where he left his own book. This interaction with Pierre bothers Dallas. Is it because we aren't supposed to be reading and now his secret is out? Or is it that Pierre used this opportunity to give Dallas a hard time? When Dallas describes the confrontation with Pierre to Jonas, he seems to be expecting Jonas to make it all better. Instead, Jonas also challenges poor Dallas. He answers in his singsong voice, "Well, you fooled him, didn't you?" My laughter at Jonas's sense of the absurd only adds to Dallas's look of growing bewilderment.

On exeat days, Jonas and I continue taking walks down the back roads. He always carries his rucksack filled with food and books, some classics by authors like C.S. Lewis and some I've never heard of before, novels, poetry, and expository tomes. The Midlands landscape is flawless—butter-colored stone villages roofed in slate or thatch, immaculate gardens spilling over

with flowers, and open fields so tidy that you know there has
been human contact with every inch of ground.

We never tire of walking through villages with names that
differentiate England from America: Chipping Camden, Wol-
ford, Bourton-on-the-Water, North Leach, Cirencester. In contrast, I never before realized how many Native American names
we have taken as our own throughout the U.S. Their sound has
its own unique music—Manitowoc, Iowa, Michigan, Penobscot,
Wyoming, Utah, Mississippi, Shawnee, Apache, Connecticut,
Cheyenne, Alaska, Potomac, Shenandoah, Milwaukee, Chicago.

Five or six months into the course, I go through a cycle for a
couple of weeks of cutting certain classes, mostly practical
work, art and psychology. Still attending Morning Exercise,
Movements, house duty, and classes or lectures presented by
Mr. B, I feel guilty more than disconnected.

One morning, instead of going to our duties, Jonas invites
me to sit in a chair in his dorm so that he can give me a shoulder
rub. After only a few minutes of this pleasure, we hear footsteps
in the hall coming closer to the room. I fear it is Mr. B. What
if he should step through the doorway and ask me to leave the
school? What would I do? I keep hoping the person is going to
walk past the room, but, no, the steps halt at the doorway. Forgetting to breathe, we wait.

In walks Giselle, that day's house supervisor. I remind
myself to inhale.

"I've been looking for you," she says to Jonas. "Would you
please get to your job?" She doesn't say anything to me. He and
I are no longer in the same group.

Jonas doesn't stop rubbing my shoulders. He just smiles at her and answers in an accommodating tone, "I'll be right there." Giselle squares her position and stands facing him with her hands on her hips. Jonas leans toward my ear and speaks as if she is no longer there,

"She's always so nice to me."

GETTING CAUGHT IS THE MOTHER OF INVENTION.

Robert Byrne

It is a rare two-day exeat, and Jonas and I decide to take a bus to a village half-a-day's distance away and then begin walking. Late in the afternoon, it starts raining just as we enter a residential area on the edge of Cambridge. There are homes everywhere, but no inns or campgrounds to be seen.

As we stand on the sidewalk discussing where to look for shelter, a middle-aged couple pulls up beside us in the English equivalent of a Lincoln Town Car. The woman does all the talking.

"We've been watching you," she says. "You remind us of our own children away at school and not much younger than you. Would you come out of the rain, stay with us overnight, and have a good hot breakfast?"

I sense they are actually shy and maybe even more fearful of strangers than I am, so they prompt our agreement. They infer a sympathetic magic assuring themselves that their children will be recipients of parallel kindnesses when they travel. We are soon warm and dry, filling up on tea and biscuits, and shown a cushy bed piled with comforters. After a good night's sleep and a hearty English breakfast of bacon, eggs, and scones, we take our leave to explore some of Cambridge's esteemed buildings including the grand dining hall built with oak beams hundreds of years old. Well after lunch we catch a bus back to Sherborne, arriving in time for dinner.

Days later I am telling Mick about the next set of oak beams to be used at Cambridge. The trees are still growing, planted 200 years ago in preparation for the time when they will be needed. Suddenly Mick insists on leading me out from the steamy kitchen to show me something. And I'm always up for one of his little ventures.

"Have you seen the Great Cypress?" he asks. "They say it was brought back from the Crusades over 700 years ago!"

Mick's excitement is as fresh as if he had just discovered the tree. Once out of the building, I have to run across the lawn to keep up with his increasing pace. Around a corner of the manor, he comes to a halt and looks straight up. When I arrive at his side, I bend my head all the way back, too. It's necessary in order to have any sense of the tree. At human level, only the immense trunk, straight as a telephone pole, but a dozen times wider, can be seen. If the two of us were standing on opposite sides of it, we would have been unable to touch each other's fingertips. I do not find it beautiful; I'm paying attention only because of Mick's excitement. The tree feels to me like Sherborne, reaching for the sky, no softness, the lowest branches stories above our heads. I don't feel like I can make contact with it despite its huge trunk soaring out of the ground right beside me.

During a lunch hour walk, Jonas takes me to visit a different tree that he has found. He is pulling me, urgent to go while I stumble, uncomfortable with the knowledge that we are going off the property, which isn't condoned. We have to climb a fence, meaning we are trespassing. All my little fears are grabbing at the back of my jacket as I trip along, though our brief junket doesn't require going more than twenty yards into the neighbor's copse.

When Jonas stops, I stand dumbfounded, trying to understand the maze in front of me. My eyes dart around looking at a dozen trunk-like, almost horizontal limbs close to the ground, then follow each of them back to a central location from which they originate. One after another, covered with light gray bark, my eyes follow them outward again. Each one runs almost horizontal to the ground for about fifteen or twenty feet before dipping down into the dirt, only to rise again out of the earth several feet later, the tips reaching out toward us.

"Come here," it beckons. "Crawl into my arms. I'll protect you."

I think of it as the Great Mother tree. Did Jonas call it that or is it just an indisputable fact?

When we are out there on another occasion, Jonas and I each pick a branch and snuggle into a spot that allows us to lean back against the central trunk where we sit in silence for a long time. When we descend, Jonas roars as he comes at me,

"This is how a bear attacks!"

I step back as he lunges. We both lose our balance to fall down laughing, cushioned by the thick overgrown winter grass. We lie together in silence until the damp chill of the ground permeates the turf and our clothing.

I visit the tree by myself on occasion. Being with it might provide a better Morning Exercise for me than what happens in the ballroom. However, since I still try to be a good student, I reject that option as quickly as it occurs to me.

In February we are given the opportunity to purchase a series of ten Alexander Technique lessons. The teachers will come to Sherborne and provide individual appointments with those who sign up. I'm told that the Technique is helpful for learning how to manage chronic back problems or any physical difficulties that arise from repetitive movement. Practitioners say that a person can learn to eliminate tension and pain by changing the habits of how one uses one's muscles. Years ago, when F.M. Alexander, the originator, first shared his technique, musicians, singers, and actors had flocked to him. I sign up.

The Alexander Lesson always leaves me feeling relaxed though I can't quite comprehend how it happens. The teacher has me sit or lie down and moves each limb for me, reminding me to let her do it. She also assists in moving me to a seated or a standing position. My job is to allow her to direct the movement. It sounds simple enough. She always gives me feedback that lets me know whether I succeed in allowing that guidance or not. Still, I am not yet able to consistently discern for myself whether I've done it.

Lessons are scheduled throughout the day to accommodate the teachers' limited time at Sherborne. One day when I can't bear another moment of history class, I leave Dick's lecture right in the middle of it by making great show of looking at someone else's watch followed by an expression of surprise on my face. I pretend to have an Alexander appointment that I've almost missed but remembered in the nick of time. My unplanned duplicity astonishes me. I guess I am learning something about myself. I thought I was too shy to act for an audience. Sorry to be dishonest yet so glad to have found a way to leave.

HONESTY IS THE BEST IMAGE.

Tom Wilson

23 ❧ LOOSE ENDS

> *We cannot exist without our enemies. They are more necessary to us than our friends. If there were no denying force, our own affirmation would dwindle. What are we if we only love our friends? Nothing at all. There is no affirmation in that. It is automatic.*

JG Bennett

In the middle of February, Mr. B has a meeting with all of the students. He asks us to observe ourselves and tell him at our next meeting what we think is our chief feature. He says that chief feature is something that Gurdjieff had often talked about with his students, describing it as the organizing principle of the personality, something which we are unable to see in ourselves but which is apparent to everyone else. This is another one of those concepts that seem to provide ammunition for the students to use against each other whenever they feel cross. "Well, you always do things like that," a student snaps. "It's your chief feature."

In contrast to the students who speak of it only in the negative, Mr. Bennett says, "Chief feature is essential to the person;

but like a double-edged sword, although it often trips him up it also gives him an advantage—a talent or a gift." He encourages us to meditate on personality and essence, to try seeing the relationship between them and chief feature.

Mr. B says, "Personality is like a shadow in that it cannot exist independently."

During a Zikr we are asked to meditate on essence. I have a vision:

I see a banana being peeled, revealing . . . a banana!

I interpret the image to mean that the fruit has skin, like personality, which is separate and thin yet reflects without being identical to the essential meat in form and color.

We gather again in the downstairs library for another chief feature meeting. After the initial long silence, Mr. B asks each of us to make a statement about our own chief feature. Everyone takes a turn without Mr. B commenting. Since he warned us last meeting that we all have to speak, I pressed myself to find something to say.

"I have a habit of seeing everything in black or white. If one person is rude to me, I feel at that moment as if I can't get along with anyone."

Jonas says, "I know I help people see themselves in a new way by not interfering with them, by not being there. The down side is that I can't bring myself to be present enough to reveal anything about myself." I don't recognize Jonas as not revealing himself. He's so full of inconsistencies, it just appears to me that contradictions define him, and that he tolerates his own and everyone else's.

After listening to us all, Mr. B says, "No one has gotten it right. Everyone is attuned to secondary characteristics."

During the next lecture, Mr. B discusses the chief feature of certain individuals by name. This is something he's never done before and which seems unduly harsh, maybe even humiliating. When he refers to Jonas being a ghost, it rings a bell of familiarity, yet still remains a puzzle. Maybe I'm not seeing all of him. I'm so appalled by Mr. B naming specific people that I don't remember anything he says about anyone besides Jonas.

Mr. B also informs us that everyone is scheduled over the next two weeks to see him for a private meeting. Previously he met with anyone who requested an appointment. However, there are probably a number of us who think we never have a good enough reason to bother him. By scheduling appointments, he makes sure we all have the opportunity to speak with him alone.

In preparation for the individual meetings, relating to the concept of chief feature, Mr. Bennett says, "I want you to observe, during Morning Exercise and at other times of the day, the response of your latifas or sacred impulses of Wish, Hope, Belief, and Will to see whether you are able to distinguish the varying degree of their strengths." When someone asks about the latifah of love, Mr. B says, "I think it is better left out right now."

Today is my private appointment with Mr. B. and I'm shaky on the way to his apartment, unsure of having any meaningful observation to bring to him. I'm so intimidated by being with him in private that I don't have any sense of the furnishings or décor around us. I'm seated and so is he. Perhaps to start me talking, he asks me what my purpose was in coming to Sherborne.

I tell him, "I'd had such a strong feeling that something was afoot in the world, that there is a big change about to happen. When I'd told June Singer, my Jungian analyst, about the feeling, she had a different view. She said it's only me who was changing."

Mr. B gives his head a little shake, as if not agreeing with her. Then he turns to the reason for our meeting, the sacred impulses. Although we've already done several variations of Morning Exercises focusing on them I can't observe or sense any difference in their strength. All I know is how often in my life I've felt hopeless, so when he asks what I've detected I give him my best guess.

"I think Hope is the weak one."

Without debate or explanation, he says, "Put your attention on the impulse of Belief whenever you have a negative thought." He adds, "In the next phase of work here, you will get rid of the separation between yourself and others."

Taking barely a second to give his words thought, I blurt out, "I don't understand the language at Sherborne. It doesn't resonate with me. It just doesn't feel right here." He doesn't try to find out more, explain anything, change my mind, or instruct me. Whatever he says leaves me with the feeling that he's heard me and that we'll see what happens. He also says, "Your conversation with June Singer is the most interesting thing you've told me."

After the meeting, I can't let go of his talking to me about Belief. Why Belief? I keep asking myself. I try to rationalize why Hope may not have been right. I do always keep on trying, even when I think everything is hopeless. *Could* the real issue be Belief? Sometimes when I say 'I Believe,' the truth of it brings tears to my eyes. More often, when I say 'I Believe,' another voice says, 'I do not.' Then I repeat, 'I Believe,' to counter it, but I don't really believe that voice.

Jonas reminds me that he and I had been talking about Joshua in the bible and the quote " . . . as I was with Moses, so I will be with thee: I will not fail thee, nor forsake thee . . . Have I not commanded thee? Be strong and of good courage: be not afraid, neither be thou dismayed: for the Lord thy God is with thee whithersoever thou goest." Despite having no sense of God, the words impart some glimmer of Hope . . . or is it Belief?

I'm reminded of Brother Lawrence's *The Practice of the Presence of God*, the one slim book I've read in full since arriving here—and his devotion to remembering the Presence. The synchronous reminders of not being alone in the universe give me comfort and, for the moment, keep me moving along. I *want* to Believe. I Believe other people's experiences of the spiritual world. But what about my own?

The children here at Sherborne are getting more mischievous, acting out and making demands. Maybe it's wintertime cabin fever, or are they, too, suffering from not receiving enough good will? A number of them come down with the current local epidemic—mumps. When I learn about the illness I wonder if a general malaise is why I had slept a day away the previous week.

In the last week of February, I awaken in the middle of the night knowing I'm delirious, seeing red outlines of devil faces floating in front of me. For a few minutes, I blink and watch them come and go. My neck feels sore, but much worse is the pain down the back of my legs, which no change of position, no tossing or turning alleviates. Moaning, because it feels better than not moaning, I don't comprehend that there might be something else to do.

None of my roommates rouse, but Mayvor from the connecting dorm comes in to look me over. She is the Swedish woman whom we believe to be recovering from drug addiction. She limps from a gunshot wound to her foot, a memento of her travels in the Middle East. She had told me, "There's been a lot of violence in my life."

She looks chronically disheveled, but she's interesting and humorous, and I admire her ability to take no notice of expectations. We never know if she's going to show up for classes or her assigned duties, and Mr. B is always inquiring after her. She is the last person I would have expected to come to my bedside.

THE ONLY COMPLETELY CONSISTENT PEOPLE ARE THE DEAD.

Aldous Huxley

Mayvor bends over me and asks with concern, "What is wrong?"

"Pain down the backs of my legs. I can't get it to stop."

"I will bring you something to help."

After she's gone, I manage to think, What could possibly help?

Barefoot and wearing pink baby doll pajamas, she makes the icy journey down the long unheated halls to the cold stone kitchen. She procures a hot water bottle, boils water, and returns to place it on my lower back. The pain subsides immediately, and like magic, I fall asleep. In the morning, I cannot make it out of bed. When it is discovered that I am a no-show for breakfast, the officials are sent to check on me. I struggle to open an eye at the sound of voices surrounding me. Mary-of-the-Kitchen and several other faces are hovering.

"Well, it doesn't look like she's faking it," Mary says. "Look at the right side of her neck and cheek. All swollen."

I have a right hand mump, and mostly I drift into some undefined darkness for hours at a time. Jonas pops in at least six times during the day. He heats the hot water bottle several times, lights a fire, reads to me, brings me flowers, oranges, apples, yogurt from the milkman, books, wood for the fire, an extra blanket, and sweetness. I dream:

> Jonas's attention to the frightened parakeet has made it much less fearful. It flies to us and it didn't used to go to anyone, even to my parents who took care of it for years.

Two days later, Jonas is still bringing me meals and heats up the hot water bottle. I'm continuing to run a fever, but I'm finally able to sit up and have a conversation.

"Mary was so mean," I tell him. "She was head of the party sent to investigate. When she saw my face, she said, 'Well, at least she isn't faking,' as if I would have." I say this with conviction because I've completely forgotten about my duplicitous trick to leave history class.

"You're lying," Jonas says, "Mary wouldn't talk like that."

Lying! A seesaw begins. All the attention and love alternates with . . . what to call it . . . hostility? Now I think he's being mean, too. I long for my girlfriends in Chicago—Chris and Stef, June Singer, the Jungian therapist, and Lynn Ellen, my first niece. I wish I could hold my brother and sister-in-law's new baby, Tricia. Jonas slips out of the room while I'm wishing.

A few days later, he shows up again around mid-morning.

"I'm so burdened by the course," he says. "Sometimes I just can't distinguish between my own negativity and what's emanating from the school."

"I agree. It's so depressing to feel that none of our observations are correct, none of our efforts are the right kind, and that I'm unable to do Morning Exercise or meditate."

"But, somehow this is the kind of place we all thought we needed," Jonas says.

He's right! Nothing different from Sherborne would have been acceptable to me. Only a couple of months ago, I wrote a post card to my cousin and her husband saying: This is just the only place I could be right now. It is perfect.

All I know now is that Sherborne is not my destination. Reminded of choosing to come here makes it possible for me to accept partial responsibility for my state. I had wanted a disciplined environment, spiritual goals, a serious introduction to spiritual activity. I hadn't wanted organized religion, robes, or anything outward that would invite reactions from the ordinary world. Nor did I want the ordinary world. This reassurance, however, still does not dissolve my dis-ease with the place.

During the illness, I vacillate from feeling hopeless to having juicy fantasies of making a trip home to be with friends and relatives, then thinking that home, too, is nowhere to go. I must remain at Sherborne, my work here unfinished, maybe not even begun.

I note another dream I remember from these days of semi-consciousness:

> There are lambkins, not from the sheep at Sherborne but brought in from elsewhere because I am too impatient to wait for ones to be born here.

Several more days pass without my knowing the time or day. This must be the sickest I've been since childhood. Someone tells me that nineteen Sherborne students are ill. Mumps is a severe virus in adults, affecting the glands and sometimes leading to reproductive complications. Most people are immune from having had it in childhood. I'm surprised that so many of us never had mumps. When I was little, many children around me had been sick with it, even my closest friend.

Dick, the frail teacher of history and psychology, visits me a week after I've fallen ill. He comes to explain the new Theme and Morning Exercise. I blather about my mental state, which isn't very lucid.

"Try not to identify with the state you're in," he needs to remind me several times, "You're ill." Around here too many people use jargon as an impatient reprimand, but he is gentle and concerned. I remember the time before Sherborne when I had been able to maintain some equilibrium. Before leaving, he bends over to give me a fatherly hug.

"Bless you," he says, this simple tenderness imbuing me with a feeling of Hope . . . or, I have to ask myself again, could it be Belief?

For treatment of the mumps, I am given my first homeopathic remedy, Belladonna. By the end of the week, I have enough energy to attend an occasional meeting. I choose to go to Theme discussion on Friday, and I remember Mr. B saying, "Sometimes the soul hungers for reality and there is nothing for it to eat; so all it can do is eat you."

Within a couple of weeks, I recover to full time participation. Only one small gland remains swollen on the right side of the back of my neck.

The next Theme, 'Intention,' Mr. B describes as being related to the words 'in tension.' "It is the state of tension caused by the disparity between our ideal state and our present state of being," he says. He also speaks about the difference between intentional and voluntary suffering, a subject returned to many times. His commanding and mellifluous inflection makes me want to agree with what he is saying whether I understand it or not.

"We all have experienced voluntary suffering where we work for a reward. We train for a marathon in order to win the race. We study for the test to get a good grade."

He discusses how every living thing must work to live.

"Even plants exert themselves. Yet the efforts we must make in order to survive are not conscious. It does not become conscious until the labor is made without working for reward. Conscious labor and intentional suffering is connected to serving the future. Parenthood is an example of intentional suffering. You must do what is needed; yet you do this without regard to what the fruits of your labor do for you. You are content that others will reap the reward of your efforts."

THERE ARE TIMES WHEN PARENTHOOD SEEMS NOTHING
BUT FEEDING THE MOUTH THAT BITES YOU.

Peter De Vries

In relation to conscious labor and intentional suffering, Mr. B devotes another lecture to the topic of air, encouraging us to meditate on its qualities.

"Air is endless, its molecules so dispersed that it seems not to be there. It has no boundaries, moving freely through the universe. All living creatures breathe the same air. It surrounds us, giving of itself without discrimination. Air makes life possible, transmitting sound and water, providing protection from harmful radiation while allowing for beneficial radiation. Air is li itless in its generosity, and we are surrounded by this spiritual quality." This is one of those lectures that sends rays of heavenly light into the dark downstairs library. I must be recovering for I'm actually able to carry some of his words out of the room with me. His observations about the qualities of air awaken gratefulness.

I'm not so sure about the virtues of suffering. Just a few years before Sherborne, I had begun to discover that joy and not the stern concept of endless efforts inspires a growing acceptance of life's vicissitudes. I can't get the Work language to meld with my previous, significant personal experiences. I attribute part of my distaste for the language to its frankness. For example, Mr. Bennett says, "It is a sin to doubt." He explains that doubting comes from egoism and is harmful in its origin and in its result.

"It is not necessary to doubt because it is not necessary to have certainty." As Mr. B delves into a topic, his meanings always make sense. Yet the choices of words still have the feeling of a British keep-a-stiff-upper-lip judgment that our emotions are essentially negative and that nothing but painful efforts can save us.

In a long night of dreams, I see images of Chicago, a jazz singing child, the child being forced to face the public, a threatening man, different streets with the air of deprivation, and a feeling of so much complexity that it is overwhelming:

> A young woman working in a restaurant that I enter asks me if the paper I'm carrying is Benedictine. No, but I was just looking at one, I tell her. This is sheet music. I realize I'm out quite late compared to my usual time of 9:00 p.m. I tell her I have been in England and mention Mr. Bennett and the school. She says to me, Us old Turks want to do everything again, don't we? There is a feeling of camaraderie. I tell her the school will go for five years altogether. She still has time to sign on. She describes to me an exercise she was taught by the restaurant manager to provide energy when she is tired. It is a sensing exercise. She breathes deeply, walks, and each time she smiles, she does so for a longer period of time.

Jonas's new attitude toward me had not been a feverish dream, disappearing with my returning health. He's become unpredictable—one moment sweet, the next, malicious. Once again, I throw the I Ching coins, seeking guidance to lessen the pain. It works out to 30, The Clinging, Fire. "It is the same in the life of man. In order that his psychic nature may be transfigured and attain influence on earth, it must cling to the forces of spiritual life." I take it to mean that I need to put my belief into the spiritual, not in attachment to another person.

24 ∾ RECOVERY

We have to be able to tolerate other people, tolerate them totally, not just externally but truly accepting other people as they are and not attempting to impose ourselves on them.

JG Bennett

Almost a month after I'd been sick, Mr. B speaks of the Theme 'breathing.' He says it is important not to interfere with breath, that time is breath, that you are out of the time experience when you stop breathing. He says, "The Zikr breathing works on us despite our mental activities and chatter. We cannot be aware of how it works on us." How are we to do the Zikr breathing pattern of a single inhalation and three exhalations yet not interfere with breathing? It's another thing I don't understand or ask about.

Morning Exercise calls for expanding the present moment. We alternate between the recent past and the near future, more distant past and more distant future until the ever-enlarging time increments include our own birth and the time of our death. The ability to feel an expanded sense of time is reassuring.

After recovering much of my physical energy following the mumps, I involve myself in the daily schedule again—house duties, classes, meditations, and Movements. However, when I missed out on learning a new complex Movement, I'm unable to pick it up in class, and I never make an effort to learn it outside of class. In fact, I continue to feel a bit detached from all the activities, even as I participate. Something about the distance feels like a good thing, like having gotten off a runaway train.

Within a period of days several teachers bring up the subject of my passivity. I can see some of it and must ask myself again if I have any reasons of my own for doing anything. If I can't find a purpose for an activity, am I able to do it as an act of devotion or for the sake of experimentation? Only today, weeks since being ill do I realize that I have not once remembered to put my attention on the "Belief" latifa as Mr. B suggested during the personal appointment.

Anna, our most constant current Movements teacher, also assesses that I am too passive in class. In this case, I cannot recognize it. Movements usually energizes me, but her class feels like walking into a black hole that sucks my light. I attribute the unexpected drain to *her* lack of energy. Who knows who is right?

On Saturday, the last day of March, I am appointed house supervisor, and we're having a work weekend. While feeling up for it, I'm also cautious, wanting to protect my newly returned energy. Again, we expect about two hundred guests. The air is electric with the excitement of preparing for so many visitors. Servers setting up for lunch seek me for direction in rearranging tables in the dining room. We spend a good amount of time experimenting with several options before determining which groupings to use. After that is settled, I think it is a good time to take five minutes to just sit and breathe, to get myself centered for the rest of our long busy day. I let one of the servers know that I am going to sit in my room.

"I'll be back within ten minutes," I tell her.

A few minutes after sitting down on the edge of my bed, Mrs. B, wearing her usual sensible shoes and colorless skirt and blouse bursts through the door. Her sandy hair is flying in wisps as if it is trying to keep up with her, and she's out of breath.

"Where have you been? Everybody's been looking for you."

She's never even talked to me before. And how did she find me so fast if no one knew where I was?

"You can't simply leave your post whenever you feel like it and abandon everything when so much needs to be done!"

"I just got here. I told Cindy where I was going. I needed to re-energize."

"That's not acceptable! Go back right now and do what you're supposed to be doing."

Like a shamed dog, I cower back to the bustle. Hours later in the day, I notice Mr. Bennett across the dining hall and cringe when he catches sight of me. He makes a beeline in my direction.

"That was very irresponsible of you!" he says, as if we were in the middle of a conversation about my faux pas. It's obvious Mrs. B reported me. While their complaints are exaggerated, I also have the feeling that the rash of recent criticism has more to do with my growing ability to bear it—perhaps the result of my increased detachment—than with the enormity of my blunders.

IF YOU CAN'T BE A GOOD EXAMPLE,
THEN YOU'LL JUST HAVE TO BE A HORRIBLE WARNING.

Catherine Aird

Jonas's unpredictability continues. He invites me to be with him, but then becomes silent and morose. When I speak of the excitement in the air, he corrects me.

"It isn't excitement. It's agitation."

I'm still trying to understand what caused the sudden change. Is it my fault? He passes me in the hall and ignores me. In the evening, he seeks me out to be affectionate. The next morning when I sit next to him at breakfast, he talks with everyone at the table and then leaves without ever speaking to me. I avoid him the rest of the day to protect myself from the hurt. Then he comes looking for me in the evening, and as soon as he finds me, I am hooked on my old expectations, wanting to believe that things have returned to normal.

My reactions to Jonas's behavior are as erratic as he is. Sometimes I find him ridiculous; at other times, his distance unleashes a fit of longing to win back his concern. Another time I take little notice of what he does; the next time it happens I cry and pray for help. Two hours later we pass in the hall, and he insists on giving me a hug. Then I wonder: Did my prayer heal him? Another day, he is resting in his room when I go to see him. He greets me with, "You're making me uncomfortable," so I leave.

Discussions with him about these events lead either to instant reconciliation or painful sarcasm. A couple of days after what appears to be the latest resolution, I greet him on our way out of the building during a fire drill, and without saying a word, he walks away. I don't know what to expect. On another day I become so angry that I shove him with such vengeance that I almost knock him off his feet. Then I am sick over possessing so much rage. He puts his arm around me, walking me down the hall, and suggests we do the Zikr. Both of us quiet down and afterward we take a nap. On the next exeat, we visit St. Catherine Cathedral in Cirencester, meditate, walk a long time in a gentle rain, hitchhike a ride to the front door of Sherborne, and feel, once again, that the tensions are a thing of the past.

Almost every day after a meal or at tea, Jonas and I sit together in silence, calling it prayer. Yet, he stops hugging me when we say good night. But if I hug him, he's responsive. What does he want? Or worse, what am I willing to put up with?

It is Sunday, and we have an exeat. Axel, the visiting first year student, suggests we all go to a Friends' Meeting along with another classmate, Penny, the mother of two boys who are so fond of Jonas. Axel wants me to get to know Anya and Keld, also from the first year and owners of the rare Jacob sheep. The outing has all the elements that Jonas and I have enjoyed in the past—new people, old friends, a new place of prayer, a free and flowing day. But Jonas is hesitant; he procrastinates about giving me an answer. When I press, he says he'll feel like a third wheel.

He suggests we could hitchhike home right after the Friends' Meeting, so we don't have to be with everyone all day. It takes great resolve for me to tell him I am going to spend the day with them even if he chooses not to. He changes his mind and decides to go.

It is a crisp wintry day. A fresh falling of snow on the ground lights up with reflected color, looking orange in the sunlight and blue in the shadows.

All I write in my journal about the day is:

> You're so quick to put me aside to do what you want to do.
> And I'm so quick to put aside anything to be with you.
> I feel cheated. You feel coerced.

Had Jonas started out treating me this way, we never would have become friends. However, now that I am involved with him, I cannot accept the reality of our relationship. Although something in me begins to let go, I mostly think there must be a way to bring back the good humor.

THE TIME FOR ACTION IS PAST!
NOW IS THE TIME FOR SENSELESS BICKERING!

Ashleigh Brilliant

The combination of detachment from school and the emotional roller coaster with Jonas has me so unbalanced that instead of going to practical work this morning, I sneak away from the house and catch a bus to Cheltenham where Anya and Keld live. Throughout the day I am unable to reach them by phone. I spend the time wandering around the city not enjoying the kind of exploration that under other circumstances would have been pleasurable. Though I had intended to run away, when the afternoon sun fades I begin to doubt the logic of my plan. My guts grumble from tension, not hunger, and I become short of breath. Before the last Sherborne bound bus stops running for the night, I return to school and write myself a poem.

> If I were not
> afraid of the dark
> of new places
> of people
> of being alone
> I could love you better.
> And if I did not see
> the possibility
> of not fearing,
> it would not hurt
> so much to fear.

As we near spring break, another Theme Mr. B introduces is 'Listening.' It exaggerates all my discomforts with feeling unable to do what we are there to do. Listening to myself is painful. I hear myself complaining, challenging, denying, agreeing. I notice how, when a group of us meet strangers on exeat, they talk to the other students but not to me. I often interrupt people by expressing enthusiasm about what they're saying, thinking to bring them closer, and instead they stop speaking. I wasn't listening.

When Mr. B finished reading *Beelzebub* to us during the evening reading, he had begun reading the sacred Hindu scripture the *Bhagavad-Gita*. At the Theme meeting, Jim asks Mr. B, "What good is it to listen to you read the *Bhagavad-Gita* to us if I can't understand what I'm hearing?"

"At least it predisposes us to new ideas," Mr. B answers.

I think back to the first time I read a full-length adult level book, *Pilgrim's Progress*, when I was in high school. I didn't like it. I thought it trite, yet persevered because something about the subject matter of seeking resonated within me. Maybe the story, corny as it seemed, reawakened my childhood aspiration for spiritual understanding.

At that time, I began to feel a connection to spiritual life by working with my dreams. I studied them on my own, and then for psychology class in college, I wrote a term paper using my own dreams to explore content, context, feeling, meaning, and interpretation. I introduced myself to CG Jung. His propensity for dealing with historical works of art as well as imagery arising from the unconscious in general spoke to me in a way I had not discovered elsewhere.

A good portion of the journal I keep here at Sherborne is taken up in writing dreams though I am too preoccupied with our daily schedule to work with them. We are told the Fourth Way frowns on dreams. They are the shit of the mind, needing regular excretion.

At this point I've been writing down my dreams for about fifteen years, working with them on my own, with therapists, and most recently with Jung's student, June Singer, author of *Boundaries of the Soul*. In my experience, dreams are of all sorts—garbage disposal, assessing experiences, practical guidance for daily life, healing and spirituality. Nevertheless, I rarely make use of them now at a time when they could be most helpful. I have lost my moorings.

While I'm overwhelmed by the intensity of all the exercises and practices, at least the predictable rhythm of tasks and classes grounds me. My finding the schedule so tedious finally begins to dissipate. Maybe that's what the sense of detachment is about. My body is more often willing to do tasks I do not like doing. I can almost enjoy the body's determination to go about its business fulfilling them.

While I continue to struggle with Sherborne's language, during teatime I copy long quotes from a book called *Mother of Carmel (St. Teresa of Jesus)* by Peers. Theresa tells of feeling only half-converted for almost twenty years, calling herself a plant of slow growth and in need of a great deal of watering. The book describes how beginners at prayer without vision, mystical experience, or emotional exaltation find it "a great labor, because they have been accustomed to a life of distraction." If she took so long to get it, maybe my own journey is not so bad.

No vision comes to strengthen Theresa and her one comfort is found in some words that are borne into her consciousness one day when she is in a "terrible state of exhaustion:

'Be not afraid, daughter, for it is I and I will not forsake thee: fear not.'"

There are those words again. "Be not afraid, for I am with you." So like the promise through Joshua in the bible. I'm not the only one bewildered by Belief.

My detached state continues right up to spring break at Easter in mid-April. Despite the ongoing melodrama, Jonas and I plan to take a vacation together. Robert and Penny, who had gone with Axel and us to the Friends' Meeting, loan us their car and the family tent. As if the auto were a large rucksack, Jonas crams it full of groceries, a Coleman stove, the ancient weighty tent, water, and books. Anticipating the open countryside, we travel north,

What began as a sunny afternoon grows dark with an ominous sky. The weather turns brisk and the wind jostles the car so badly that we struggle to keep it on the road. We decide to cut the travel short and set up camp. Not another soul is at the campgrounds. By this time, the wind is blowing in forty-mile-per-hour gusts, yanking the heavy old canvas out of our hands. It begins to rain and the temperature drops. We're freezing while tussling the tent into submission, amazing ourselves that we're able to figure out what's supposed to go where. With the tent set up, our clothing soaked, and the temperature falling, triumph is all the sweeter when we finally crawl inside, light the stove and cook ourselves a hot meal. Like our relationship, the challenges seem unavoidable and moments of quiet and warmth a worthwhile reward. I've recovered from the mumps, from the pace of the school, but not yet from Jonas.

IV
THE ESOTERIC PHASE:
MANIFESTATION

Mid-April to Mid-September, 1973

25 ❧ QUESTIONS

One must learn to use life as one's teacher. We have
to learn from life for our own being, for our own
transformation.

JG Bennett

In the downstairs library Mr. Bennett gives a series of lectures to prepare us for the last phase of the course. As usual, most of us sit on cushions on the floor while the older people sit on the few chairs in the room. He reminds us of the parable of making bread. Mr. B says, "When looking at the last stage of the process, the esoteric, it is not the baking of the bread that is the last step. The last phase comes when we are assimilating it as food. It is only then it serves its purpose, feeding the community. Likewise, in terms of human transformation, the esoteric phase is the birth of the spiritual man. Although it is likely that most of you will not achieve such a state of being while you are here, we should understand that the transformed person is one who becomes the source of Work for himself and through which the Work flows into the world for the sake of others. During this last stage of our studies at Sherborne, you will be more involved with activities that will give you the opportunity to manifest something to benefit the greater community."

To help us understand the underlying laws of the universe regarding the process of transformation, Mr. B uses the symbol of the enneagram. He applies it to the most concrete of activities, such as preparing a meal, and to the most subtle of processes,

THE KITCHEN AS A COSMOS

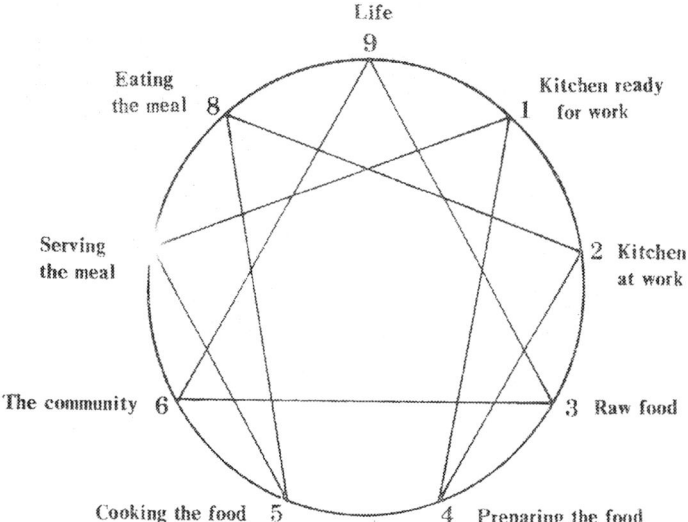

such as the transformation of man's spirit, a task required for evolving the life of the universe.

He explains that, "By comprehending the pattern demonstrated by the symbol, we follow the steps depicted at each point, not only in numerical order to learn how events unfold, but to identify how and why they go wrong."

He compares the figure to music, to notes and the intervals between, also how the reality we live in is not linear and how the enneagram can also guide our perceptions of the non-linear universe. The structure reflects the working of cosmic laws, of three processes: function, being, and will, and their interdependence. He speaks of the significance of the six-sided figure 1, 4, 2, 8, 5, 7 and the three-sided 9, 3, and 6. At moments, Mr. B conveys truths about the preparation of the kitchen, the food, and the cook's mind. While the cerebral exercise is elegant, I find it all complex beyond my interest, and I cannot stay with it.

One of several 'manifesting' activities during the last third of the year is for each of us to complete a six-week Decision exercise. Someone asks, "How do we figure out whether a project will take six-weeks?"

Mr. B assures us, "The only way to know how to calculate the length of time needed for a long-term project is to do it. With experience, you'll get better at estimating." The dilemma of estimating the time needed reminds me of learning to draw at the School of the Art Institute. As beginners, we would draw the figure beginning with the head, and by the time we got down to the feet, we'd run out of paper. With practice, we learned to keep the whole figure in sight, breaking it up into smaller sections, working the details only within the larger context by returning repeatedly to the whole in order to maintain the proportions. The advanced students spent most of their time studying the subject, only rarely looking down to work their drawings.

A long-term Decision has already caught my attention. The fireplace in my dorm had once been lined with ceramic tiles, but all that is left is the metal backing and a few shards. What if I were to reline the fireplace? I know where to get tile. In the servery, our dinner dishes are often dropped and broken, the shards put into a bucket. I can see the design in my mind's eye. The half-inch wide blue stripe on the plate rim, broken into little arcs, would become two or three stripes along the outer-most area of the fireplace walls. The blue flowers from the center of the plate would also be rearranged in sections contrasting with all white areas. Every day I go down to the servery, collect shards from the bucket, and carry them up to my dorm.

I haven't found out about the types of materials needed to glue the ceramic pieces in place and to fill in the spaces between them, and there's no local hardware store to ask. We're always so busy I keep putting off finding an answer. Before I know it, the allotted six weeks are gone. And now we are assigned appointments for a second private meeting with Mr. Bennett.

At the appointment, we are to discuss with him how the exercise has gone. He also wants us to bring written answers to these three questions:

1. How did I work on my six-week Decision task?
2. What is my problem or how am I stuck? This needn't relate only to the task but to our process or lives at Sherborne in general.
3. What would we like to see different around Sherborne?

"Your answers," he pointed out, "might also reveal something about your chief feature."

Begun before spring break, it is now the end of April, and I dread the meeting, not knowing the consequences for not finishing the six-week decision. Another layer of clothing is not helping me stop shivering as I walk the long hall to Mr. B's office. After I'm seated, I confess that my Decision exercise is still unfinished. He registers no disappointment. Instead, he suggests I take an additional six weeks to complete the fireplace.

"Ask George to tell you what kind of glue and grout to purchase. These kinds of things are his expertise." It never occurred to me to consult George who is in charge of all our practical repair and maintenance work.

At the moment, I am eager to get on with telling Mr. B my opinion of Sherborne as he had asked us to.

"I resent you," I tell him. "I think the school is impersonal, always negative with constant warnings about our pathetic nature. I don't feel like I have anyone on the staff to talk with, no individualized counseling; and the atmosphere is so gloomy and disapproving that I've become apathetic about being here."

He looks me straight in the eye, which makes me feel sure he is listening, and says nothing to interrupt my tirade. When I'm done, we just sit in silence. I'm too nervous to remember to say the other thoughts I'd had, that I find his manner Victorian and authoritarian and in conflict with much of what he says to us about how we should treat each other.

Mr. B takes a deep breath. Then he says, "You are unable to reach out. You make demands of the world and when they aren't met, you withdraw . . . I *do* care about you."

I just ignore his saying he cares about me, and I can't accept the rest of what he says, either. I'm thinking, Reach out? Why, I have a cadre of friends here with whom I'm able to talk about most anything. And we laugh together about the predicaments we find ourselves in. What could he mean? But I don't ask.

He continues, "Do you remember some of the activities you said you wanted to participate in on your original application to Sherborne?"

Hadn't eons passed since then?

"Yes, I remember."

He has my application in his hands and is running a finger down various items as he speaks.

"Did you join the choral group?"

"I went to the first meeting, but I didn't like the kind of music they were singing so I didn't go back." It doesn't occur to me until this moment that as a participant I could have suggested other music. I always assume that when someone else is in charge, I am not allowed any input.

"What about propagating plants?" Mr. B is referring to a project outside of our daily gardening or my caring for the houseplants. He is talking about getting seedlings started for next season's vegetable garden.

"Flo is so bossy. I couldn't stand the way she hovered over my shoulder, micro-managing my every move."

"Hmmm. I see you were interested in working on a rock garden. Did you work on the one we started in January?"

"I have terrible circulation." I'm thinking about how my big toe keeps going white even when I'm in the house. Reynaud's syndrome. I panic over its numbness and pace the halls trying to get the blood moving again. To Mr. B, however, I only say, "My hands were freezing in the cold."

He doesn't get caught up in my answers, instead, seeming to conclude our talk by saying in a gentle tone, "Just go out to people and be friendly. Radiate warmth to them."

What is he talking about?

Instead of asking, I dig in my heels. I think about how all the magic in my life before Sherborne seems to have departed. Despite my inability to digest what he's saying, a tiny voice far away is whispering, "He's not talking about the times when you *do* reach out, only about the situations when you don't."

It's not true that life is one damn thing after another;
it is one damn thing over and over.

Edna St. Vincent Millay

After the meeting, I feel pained about the number of activities for which I found reasons not to participate. Hadn't the anticipation of them contributed to making Sherborne so attractive? By not initiating dialogues to address what I experience as problems, I am not honoring the other person or myself. I live in a world *expecting* my concerns to be ignored or devalued . . . and when they are, which is most of the time since I never speak up, I have no recourse.

From the moment I ask George for help, the rest of the six-week Decision project is as easy as collecting the shards had been. He tells me exactly what products I need.

Another piece of information arising from this experience is in having completed an undertaking I believed would require large blocks of time. Instead, five to fifteen minutes a day are more than sufficient. At first, I thought I had never experienced anything like that before, but of course, I have. We all have. Didn't we learn to talk, walk, write, and roller skate by practicing in small increments over a long period of time?

The long-term Decision also provides technical practice regarding Decision-making. I found a task that is related to my being plus I learned how to break it up into sensible parts. In the process, I keep returning to the goal, maintaining other activities that need to be done, and appreciate, by continuing to do them, how to create energy that supports the aim. I look forward to being able to apply this experience in the future.

George tells me that he's had a dream about me:

"We're all in a group meeting when Mr. B says, 'Some people never ask questions. In order to encourage everyone to do so I'm going to pull names out of a hat.'

"You were shaking with fear," George says, "sure he was about to pull out your name. Just before dipping his hand into the hat, you thought of a question and raised your hand. He called on you.

"Mr. B said, 'That's the best question anyone has ever asked.' Then, looking around the room he says, 'Why haven't any of you thought of that?'"

If I won't listen to my own dreams, perhaps I'll listen to someone else's. Maybe George is trying to tell me that my unspoken questions are worth airing, but before that can happen, I need to respect their validity.

26 ❧ UP THE LADDER

It one of the laws that if we wish to change we must make it possible for somebody else to change.

JG Bennett

My thinking function is beyond overload. The only thinking I'm doing is visual, no words. Images of eggs keep popping into my mind unbidden. I have accumulated a collection of black and white photos taken around the property. In my mind, each one of them begs for a sunnyside up egg—hanging on a fence, resting on the balustrade, being held in someone's hand while companions examine it, and, even, lurking behind the flora. A cheery prowling egg! Mrs. Bennett hears about the photos with eggs painted on them and asks to see them. I wonder what she is doing with them, imagining her taking them to a psychiatrist for professional evaluation.

Charts and graphs come to mind with eggs as the markers. Sometimes I copy graphs from scientific journals in the library and paint my 18 x 24 inch version of them on sheets of brown craft paper tacked up on the dormitory wall. In general, people laugh when they see them. The cartoons have an innate humorous nonsensical quality; I am sure they are keeping me sane though I don't know how.

One dorm mate, Nadine, often talks and jokes with other people, but never has much to do with me, so of course, I don't try to befriend her either. When anyone comes into our room and looks at my art, her face darkens. Today, after some visitors leave, she scowls.

"What is the meaning of this so-called art?"

"I can't explain them," I say. "The images just come to me."

She spins on her heel and marches out of the room. My answer doesn't please her.

I often come to our dorm at the end of morning tea and lie down for five or ten minutes to get past the low blood sugar shakes that always hit me that time of day. If Nadine arrives at the same time to change from her gardening clothes, she never speaks with me but on her way out slams the door as hard as she can. I assume she is protesting my lying down in the middle of the day, which is frowned upon, but neither of us brings it up for discussion. It's another instance of where I'm unwilling to confront anyone's anger or my own response to it.

Gerald, the abstract expressionist artist whom Mick introduced me to at the garage invites me to have tea with him, but instead of serving tea, he shows me prints of famous paintings, which nourish my eyes with color and composition. After displaying a stack of Matisse and Bacon reproductions, he sends me on my way with a roll of beautiful textured art paper. I don't even know if he's seen my work, but he behaves as if I'm a fellow artist.

I work on a triptych, art in three sections, which reminds me of the active, receptive, and reconciling forces so often mentioned in lectures. Three images come, camouflaging their meaning in humor. They share a similar shape. A blue Saturn with its rings is the active force; a brown bagel with lox and cream cheese peeking out from between the top and bottom halves is the receptive; and a sunnyside up egg, floating cloudlike in a blue sky is the reconciling.

After lunch, Jon the juggler intercepts me in the hall. As if to fulfill the role of divine messenger, he shows me a book called *The Millennium of Hieronymus Bosch* by Wilhelm Franger, then points to a paragraph for me to read.

" . . . the egg contains the meaning of the world; and to attain equilibrium with the world, to be attuned to its creative harmony and to make oneself an instrument of divine Nature, appeared to the community of the Free Spirit as the condition sine qua non of spiritual perfection." Another section he points to reads " . . . whose egg-like shape show it to be the germ-cell and navel of this paradisiacal world." The words seem to fit.

In keeping with the egg theme, even though Jonas and I spend less time together he still points out excerpts from books he has on hand. In *Mere Christianity* by C.S. Lewis, he shows me, "It may be hard for an egg to turn into a bird: It would be a jolly sight harder for it to learn to fly while remaining an egg. We are like eggs at present. And you cannot go indefinitely being just an ordinary decent egg. We must be hatched or go bad."

Only one of my paintings strays from the egg theme. It is a light bulb with its network of tiny filaments exposed. Rather than seeing it as the metaphor of a bright idea, I equate it with the mitochondria within a cell, the engine of minuscule transformations.

PEOPLE WHO LIKE THIS SORT OF THING WILL FIND THIS
THE SORT OF THING THEY LIKE.

Abraham Lincoln

As if to confirm the egg and germ cell images, Morning Exercise asks us to be in a collected state and to bring that state into another person. I have a sense that I can accomplish this, that being centered allows me to enter someone else's being. In another variation on the exercise, we are asked to see the whole room of people and experience: "I am they; they are I; we are the same."

Mr. B explains, "The collected state exercise is an action on our own being, enabling us to be as we should be." Although I still wonder if I'm doing these exercises correctly, I've reached a point where I simply try to do them to the best of my ability and then look back on my experience and evaluate it.

Several Themes also relate to the morning meditation, revolving around sensitivity to other people. We discuss inner considering and how we explain things to ourselves often using secondhand information or imagination. Although it is clarifying to understand the negative quality of thinking that is based on misinformation or non-information, again, the word 'imagination' is used in a pejorative way, as if its main form of expression is in gossip and half-truths. Rarely is imagination described in its function as a channel to direct knowledge through visions or other forms of 'knowing.'

Despite being uninspired by Work language and the staff's expression of scorn toward emotions, my understanding of all the ways in which we are linked to one another increases. Every aspect of our daily lives reflects the connection, and Theme observations made by the students confirm a shared experience. Whether this is the result of more opportunities to "manifest" or awareness growing from the amount of time we've been here, I cannot help but see the connections and contributions among us.

We know where our food comes from, how the soil is treated, how food is harvested, who delivers it to the kitchen, how it gets washed, how leftovers will be returned to the garden or fed to the chickens, the ways in which each of us functions. My being unable to find a broom that *I* had not put away three days before, how often someone's gift fills a need that had been left undone, experiencing the shared state of one-hundred people, admiring how the complex house kept operating during vacation with no sign-up sheet, all are microcosms of the greater world.

At Sherborne we participate in so much more of essential day-to-day processes than in our lives outside of Sherborne. In addition, we see how someone's bad mood ruins a meal or someone's good mood spills over to the rest of us. Hurt feelings destroy a project. Joy creates cooperation. Greed leaves others without bread to eat. A cook's lack of awareness in doling out dinner takes the meal away from the hardworking pot scrubber. We experience all sides; and can react badly or cope gracefully with each of them. Accumulated trash attracts rodents or, when cleaned up, contributes to the beauty and order of our environment. The limits of the school setting make these incidents so much more obvious than out in the world where the magnitude of activity allows much to go unnoticed.

Because daily activity revolves around our own care and feeding, I appreciate what it takes to accomplish these things. Every activity reveals our attitudes, how we treat each other, the planet, the universe, and ourselves. Mr. B asks us at different times to imagine what could be accomplished if people did not have the need for personal recognition or the need to indulge in discouragement. What if we would act just because we know a certain action is the right thing to do? The quality of our lives depends on our struggle with ourselves.

Another project to help us finish out the year began in mid-May. Each student teaches some topic of their expertise to the other students in their group. The projects give us a small taste of experiencing change in ourselves by helping someone else learn something new. This will continue for weeks until everyone has a turn.

Cormac shows us chancery cursive calligraphy. I practice, transforming my journal into a medieval text for about twelve pages. Mayvor teaches us to make chapatti, rolling and folding the dough with a layer of oil between every fold. They puff up when fried or baked and have a wonderful flavor. Jonas coaches our group on how to make muffins. We meet him down in the kitchen where he has laid out a variety of ingredients for us to choose from.

"You can use any kind of flour," he says. "Combine it with eggs, milk, juice or water mixed to a somewhat stiff consistency. That's really all the information you need. Any other ingredients are up to you." He points to the foods on the kitchen worktable: oil, nuts, raisins, rolled oats, and cooked pumpkin.

"Fruits and vegetables like apples, grated zucchini and carrots, or cooked squash add flavor and moisture. Baking soda or powder can make the muffins a little lighter but so do eggs, especially if you beat the whites and fold them in."

As delighted by this haphazard method as I am, Keith, an earnest mathematician-type, is affronted by Jonas' nonchalant improvisation. His questions reflect a growing anxiety.

"How much flour should I use? What measure of raisins for that amount of flour? How do I know when there's enough liquid? How many ingredients are allowed in a batch?" And finally, a thunderous, "What do you think they have recipes for?" Despite Keith's apprehension of danger, everyone's muffins come out fine.

Russ, the art teacher, and I discuss the possibility of my offering a ceramics class as my part in the teaching exercise. The way he puts it is something like, "Let's find an outlet for your passive flexibility and active inflexibility." I'm not that interested in teaching ceramics because I've done that in my life before Sherborne. However, I appreciate Russ at the moment for his generous recognition that working with clay is something I can share and for listening to my other idea. It is the first time all year that Russ and I have what I would call a conversation.

Instead of pottery, I decide to teach a variation on the fabric decorating technique called tie-dye, only we are going to tie-bleach. All we need is fabric that fades, string, and bleach. On exeat, I carry a small bottle of bleach with me to a fabric shop and draft the saleslady into cutting samples of dark colored cottons that we dip into the bleach. When I find a rich blue that bleaches out to a range of shades from white to the darkest tones, I buy enough fabric so that everyone in our group will have several eighteen-inch squares to experiment with. The long-range plan is to sew the squares into covers for our Morning Exercise cushions.

In class, I demonstrate an assortment of techniques to tie and sew the fabric so the bleach can't get to parts of it. It addition, after it is bound, we soak the fabric in water before putting it into the bleach. The wet string and thread make a better barrier than when dry. The results are beautiful. We get a wide array of patterns ranging from the easy-to-recognize flower child's bull's eye to complex rhythmic designs formed by neat pleating and tying.

The finished pieces still need to be sewn together to create cushion covers, and only one person, my dorm mate, Renee, volunteers to help. I'm disappointed by the low response. How can I accomplish the goal without more people? Nevertheless, the new buoyancy in the atmosphere, perhaps coming from nearness of completing the course, makes it possible for me to just press on. Letting go of my preconceptions about what is needed, I think instead about how to do what we can.

It is an exeat day, and rather than leave the property, stalwart Renee and I start sewing cushion covers using the same sewing machines that were used to sew Movements costumes. In less than an hour, a few students join us, at first only curious to see what we are doing, then being drawn into helping. The sides must be matched and pinned inside out. Volunteers find more sewing machines and bring them into the ballroom where we're working. Different people come and go throughout the day, again demonstrating to me how much gets done by working in increments and being open to accepting support in whatever form it presents itself. Many cushion covers are finished and over a few days more keep appearing. I complete only a few myself, yet I initiated the project and, in a way, channel the energy that brings them into existence. The covers appear like magic.

The way help arrives reminds me of situations from my pre-Sherborne art projects, though I don't think I could have put the experience into words until now. Often, the artistic objects that I wished to make required some technical skill that I didn't possess—using an electric saw, casting forms in plastic, bolting together lap joints for a two-by-four bed frame. When I tried to get help before getting started, I'd never find it, but if I just jumped in and began working, help would arrive, sometimes before I even asked for it. I've heard people say that maybe the universe wants us to make a show of faith before meeting us half way. Do I need the project to go according to my direction, or will I accept help in the form the universe provides?

THE FIRST STEP IN THE ACQUISITION OF WISDOM IS SILENCE, THE SECOND LISTENING, THE THIRD MEMORY, THE FOURTH PRACTICE, THE FIFTH TEACHING OTHERS.

Solomon Gabriol

Even now, in the last third of the course, there are still issues about food. On our applications to Sherborne, we had been offered a choice of meat or vegetarian fare. Yet Mr. Bennett lectured at intervals about vegetarian eating and how often we in the West do it only for sentimental reasons. Each time he brings up the topic, he emphasizes the negative implications and reminds us about the spiritual transformation of any food. More and more people opt out of their vegetarian diets.

As an experiment, I'd been hoping to improve my health by eating vegetarian, but as each lecture convinces more students to give it up, I've become the only vegetarian left. This is no longer a health experiment for me but only obstinacy. I think we've been manipulated. And then I sadly wonder if my stubbornness can be applied to something more uplifting.

I WAS A VEGETARIAN UNTIL I STARTED LEANING TOWARD THE SUNLIGHT.

Rita Rudner

On a related note, my roommates discover my cheese stash in the dorm, and they eat it when I'm not around. I've never discussed my low blood sugar symptoms with anyone, so they have no idea this protein is medicine for the shakes I get every morning as we are completing our work in the garden. From the time I was a child, I've had daily bouts where I felt so shaky I would have to lie down. When it gets that bad, my face goes white, and I break into a cold sweat. Sometimes the weakness is so intense it brings me to tears. The simultaneous mental confusion at those moments makes it impossible to determine whether I even need a glass of water if someone nearby observing my state asks.

In college, a friend gave me a book about nutrition. It sounded to us like my symptoms were from low blood sugar. I experimented with my diet and made great progress. Doctors had never treated or tested me for anything during all the years I told them about it. When I cut out bread to go easy on processed carbohydrates, the change was almost miraculous. I continued to practice this solution at Sherborne. However, since being here, I'm having mild bouts of weakness and shaking again and can't determine why. I almost never eat bread here and only rarely the tea biscuits.

It's taken me until now—June—only two months before the end of the course, because of frustration over the vanishing cheese, to finally go to Mrs. B and explain my health history. Sympathetic to my dilemma, she arranges for me to have yogurt every morning instead of porridge. How typical of me to wait for a crisis instead of trusting my years of experience and making suitable arrangements.

On the course, we're having some well-known visitors. Perhaps Mr. B feels that we've become civilized enough to appreciate them without being distracted from our work. Edith Wallace, a Jungian analyst presents herself as a student of Mr. Bennett's. As an artist, she creates luminous tissue paper collages and also leads us in a workshop using the same material. The abstract artwork, when examined with care, reveals subjects that occupy the unconscious of the artist. During her stay of several days, we are invited to make appointments to speak with her privately. I make one after awakening from a dream crying:

> I discover that the pet parakeet of my childhood, Twinkle, has been shut up in the freezer. I find him there and let him out.

Grief from the dream lingers all day until I speak with Edith about my response to Sherborne. "The atmosphere here inhibits my playfulness and creativity. I want the information we're given but everything is so burdensome. I'm driven to doing artwork, my main way of expressing humor and perception."

Edith says, "You won't have to live in this environment much longer. And despite the methods not being compatible with your nature, you will benefit from Mr. Bennett's genius. He's given me something I wasn't getting from Jung."

DREAMING PERMITS EACH AND EVERY ONE OF US
TO BE QUIETLY AND SAFELY INSANE
EVERY NIGHT OF OUR LIVES.

William Dement

Another eminent visitor is Idries Shah, a teacher of Middle Eastern wisdom in the form of traditional teaching stories. We are warned not to crowd him by demanding attention the way the students had done the first year, embarrassing Mr. B with their poor manners and possibly displaying how little they'd learned. Shah is a dark handsome Afghan wearing a stylish black leather jacket befitting a rock star. Many of the students are familiar with his collections of stories. Shah, like Bennett, is gifted in speaking of the ineffable, but in a different way—with more humor and sarcasm while pointing to the frailties of our human condition.

He said, "Although hearing a lecture one time or perhaps even many times can hardly substitute for being at a school and living in the presence of a teacher, such meetings can certainly prepare you for being able to benefit in the future from wisdom to which you might be exposed."

Was he saying we might have achieved very little in our time with Mr. Bennett? That Mr. B might not be a real teacher or Sherborne a real school? That we weren't properly chosen as students? My brain feels like it has been crocheted by the time he is done with us, though I am left with a now-familiar sense of his telling us how, as seekers, we tend to become attached to all the wrong things and, besides, always miss the point of what we're being shown.

27 ❧ THE FATE OF THE FÊTE

All real enjoyment is as good, from the point of view
of energy production and conservation, as suffering.

JG Bennett

The last phase of the course is filled with a new energy, a sense of promise, though the core of our daily schedule has not changed. What a relief! We continue our usual activities of housework, gardening, Theme, Movements, and the evening reading. But now more of our other activities have a creative and interactional element to them. The longer days and burgeoning signs of spring appear to be earth's way of joining in on the assignment to manifest our work.

For the first time in months, out in the garden students are tossing off their down vests and jumpers, as the British call sweaters. Fewer layers of warm clothes make everyone appear to have lost anywhere from ten to thirty pounds. It has been so long since I've seen my bare arms in the light of day, that when I lay eyes on them, I feel indecently exposed.

There are trips to the garden where Mick and I search for woad, a plant once used to make the purple dye used by royalty and to see his hot-colored oriental poppies waist high tumbling over each other. Gertie, my friend with Parkinson's, and I celebrate our upcoming birthdays with little chocolate cakes from the post office. We've been missing such ordinary pleasures.

I tell Gertie that what feels like another birthday present, is a coming visit from my Jungian analyst, June Singer. I am touched that she suggested coming here, for my own parents visited me only once since I've lived away from them, and that was when I was still in Chicago. She is coming for three days, which include June 8, Mr. Bennett's 75th birthday and my 31st. And I'm still wondering if our shared birthday reflects having anything in common with him.

When] ie Singer arrives, Mr. B treats her as if she were a parent visiting, as several have during the year. I'm delighted that he invites her to observe classes and to talk with him about the school, even though their time together cuts into the time I might have had with her.

Also reflecting the season, Lena and Fred, two students on the course, announce their impending marriage. The wedding becomes a feast day, *de rigueur* for any celebration at Sherborne. Following the ceremony, everyone stands on the front steps in the blinding sun to pose for group photos.

The bride's white gown is like a fitted monk's robe with a hood hanging down her back. Her black hair and bouquet of red roses provide striking punctuation. It's an idyllic day of sunshine, blue skies, and smiling faces as we students leisurely alternate between household duties, rambling in the gardens, and watching the children play.

For a new Theme, Mr. B presents 'personality.'

"Personality reflects our training," he says, "our learned ways useful for participating in the surrounding environment. It's a mechanism we need in order to function in society."

I think of how attracted I had been to Jonas' personality. He had such a quirky sense of humor that seemed perceptive and always made me laugh.

Despite Mr. B's explanation of its positive role, I most often hear personality spoken about by the old students with derision, not compassion.

The next week Mr. Bennett speaks about false personality that tries to pass itself off as authentic, but which is actually a multiplicity of contradictions. Is that what I've been seeing in Jonas? How am I supposed to tell the difference between true and false? And from which part of me are my responses coming?

My struggle with truth seeking, however, is short-lived, taking a back seat to delight in the weather, which is making its own efforts to warm up. Jonas, too, still runs cold and hot, and although the intensity between us has lessened, we still spend some time together. On a day I realize I've not seen him anywhere I look for him and find him in the nest, ill. When I visit him again before the reading he is all smiling and loving. He asks me to read to him, trim his hair, and bring him a hot water bottle. I notice he's received a letter from home, his friend, Allison, but he doesn't offer to read it to me the way he would in the past.

On the next exeat, we get hold of a map of walking paths that, used once a year, remain open to the public even though they're on private property. The day is mellow, and the path we choose is so ancient, left from the Roman invasion, that it is worn deep into the ground. We often have to climb the sides of the trench to gaze upon the greening fields.

On the following exeat which is for two days, Jonas and I go to Guy and Veronica's house. They're longtime students of Mr. Bennett's whom we met at Sherborne during a couple of the work weekends. We spend a lot of time gardening in the sun and I enjoy putting up a bookshelf for Veronica.

Guy is a quiet white-haired gentleman, Veronica a petite fiery redhead. She and I love to laugh. I tease her into giggling beyond control by imitating her accent. She slaps my arm trying to catch her breath when I won't stop. Breathing interspersed with laughter, that's my kind of zikr.

Back in May, when our three groups had been reconfigured again, Mr. Bennett introduced the grandest project on our plate of 'manifestation' for the last third of the course. Our assignment is to orchestrate a fête to be held at Sherborne near the end of June to benefit the building fund of the local Catholic Church. Each group is given a unique role: to specialize in meditation, to perform Ibsen's *Peer Gynt*, or to present Morris Dance.

We're allowed to choose whichever group we wish, although I hear rumors that certain students had not been given their choice. I am exceptionally satisfied to have chosen and to be in the Morris Dance group. My contentment reminds me of being in the 'average' group near the beginning of the course where, when doing Movements, our group felt neither too competitive, nor too awkward. As a member of the Morris group, we can't be too quiet as in meditation nor too much the focal point of an audience as when acting in a play. The commonality of our group members springs from an easy-going playfulness. And, by the way, Jonas is on the team, too.

The traditional English village dance is said to derive from Moorish dances, each village having its own variations. Mr. B invites from the outside a traditional Morris instructor who teaches dances that are known to have originated in Sherborne village, though it's been many years since village residents danced them. Part of 'traditional' means that only the men of the group dance. The women play a supporting role—sewing costumes, tending to supplies, and baking and serving cake at the performances. Jenny and I bristle when we hear about our function.

Morris Dance is usually danced in groups of six men at a time. The costume consists of white shirts and pants, a black bowler hat, and a red sash pinned on the right hip with a rosette of red, white, and green ribbon. Each dancer carries a white handkerchief in one hand, red in the other, and wears shin pads covered with noisy bells, producing a pleasing percussion from the dancers' steps. Two men on our team play instruments, one a concertina and the other an accordion. They learn the music by following the teacher who, at first, plays fiddle until they learn the tunes.

All Morris teams dance the same steps except for the kicks and jumps that are unique to each village's style. Handkerchiefs are used for flourishes and, in some dances they use sticks to clank as the men hit them together.

Often the best dancer of the team plays the fool, weaving in and out among the dancing team members. He's knowledgeable enough to stay out of their way yet involved enough to challenge their concentration. His costume is a long patchwork vest over the same white shirt and pants everyone wears. Juggler Jon is our perfect dancing fool, though he was sure it was a mistake when he wasn't given either of his preferred group choices. A determined visit to Mr. Bennett clarified that it was not a mistake. He was chosen to work on himself, and much to our group's good fortune Jon rises to the challenge.

The dance engenders a boisterous maleness we all enjoy, directing their active energy into playful competition. Who can jump higher? Stay in the air longer? Snap his handkerchiefs with greater embellishment? They cajole and applaud each other, drawing in passers-by with an exuberance that makes everybody smile.

A paper maché horse costume worn by a team member carries a basket in its mouth to collect donations from onlookers. As put off as some of us women felt at first, as soon as we heard the music our dour mood dissipated and never returned. The tunes are unknown but with a familiar lilt to them. Everybody grins when the music starts.

When Mr. B asks us students what we think of Morris Dance, we all agree it makes us feel close to each other and more optimistic. Whether we are spectators from the other student groups or team members, the music and dance changes our states. I'm surprised that I, too, feel so close to everyone, since I've been assigned a separate task to be done during Morris practice time.

Mr. B asked if anyone knows how to throw pottery. I had been required to take pottery classes at the Art Institute, but in my perfectionist thinking, knowing I can't throw as well as the pottery majors, I don't claim expertise. Tomás, always confidant he can do anything, volunteers. However, when Russ shows me

Tomás's drooping ashtrays, I offer that I can at least make pots taller than those.

"Where I'll get stuck," I tell him, "is on the glazing," another one of those technical things that catch me up. Russ says he'll take care of that; so while the Morris team dances on the cement pad just outside the art studio, which is the old estate orangery, I am inside making a few pottery tools from twigs and wire. I throw dozens of small vase-like forms and partial forms to combine with hand building into container shapes. Rolling out the clay on burlap sacks gives it texture. Between the potter's wheel and the worktable, I form vessels that are spontaneous and playful. Russ rubs colored oxides into the textures and then glazes them with a clear shiny glaze. Not anything like what I would have done, which adds to my finding them interesting despite their dark tones.

TO INVENT, YOU NEED A GOOD IMAGINATION
AND A PILE OF JUNK.

Thomas A. Edison

Russ's girlfriend, Perdie, visits him in the art studio. She glares at me, making no greeting. She's on the staff, too, teaching psychodrama, a talent she displays daily. Whenever we have class with her she acts so irate, I'm convinced she's just had a fight with someone. Maybe she, too, feels marginalized by the attitude toward psychology, but I never think to reach out to someone who frightens me with her anger.

In the orangery, she whispers to Russ, keeping private whatever her business. I wonder if seeing him and me working together motivates her unfriendliness. If so, it's a total waste of her energy. Russ and I rarely even speak to each other; meaning, in my mind, we are getting along better than ever. At least I'm not being battered by his sarcasm.

The art studio orangery is a plant conservatory made of glass, letting in sunlight from all sides, which cheers me. The hours spent here are the most satisfying times. I'm doing something I love and, for a change, it is viewed as useful to the community. The orangery is as special to me as my other favorite place, the cloister. And the magic of pottery always awes me— clay's amazing plasticity that can imitate, in looks, any other material while it possesses the ability to be transformed into permanence by fire.

Best of all, I listen to the Morris men right outside the door, practicing and playing music. The women gather around them smiling and doing whatever tasks they're working on. To take breaks, I go out to the dancers and am welcomed to dance in place of whoever needs to catch his breath. These few weeks of light and cheery mornings filled with music, dance, and art are *my* golden age at Sherborne.

Across the lawn to one side of the estate is a copse of dark larch trees, always seeming to be in silhouette. In a photo, I place them between the camera and the House, their hanging branches framing the architecture that has lost its graceless appearance as I have become accustomed to the foreign aesthetics. Mrs. Bennett sees my black and white photo and decides to have post cards printed from it in time to be sold at the fête.

As the event draws near, many students mention having dreams about their preparations for it. It is our seminal joint venture. During the weeks of preparation the Morris group is on house duty more often than the others, yet we remain cheery, attributing our mood to the music that buoys us up each day. We are also on house duty the day of the fête, not feeling as if we're missing out on anything; Morris dance has endowed us with a miraculous state of equanimity.

On the big day each group plays its role, and we all contribute to the grand complex occasion. The Morris dancers are billed as performing the famous *Sherborne* Morris Dances in the village proper for the first time in a century, which is true, and makes us feel that we are doing something special for the village as well.

I have no idea where all the guests have come from. There's more people here than live in Sherborne village. I hear that some students are directing the parking of cars but I have no idea where that's taking place. It must be outside of the property.

Mr. B had suggested that the students make handcrafts in our spare time to be sold at the fête. As I walk through the grounds, I am amazed to discover improvised craft booths selling dozens of wooden toys, crocheted booties and hats, and the pottery I've made, some of the larger pieces crammed with living plants. People of all ages are chatting as they visit the booths, and money is changing hands. There are even donkey and pony rides with long lines of children each holding onto a parent as they wait their turn. There's so much more happening than I knew about.

In between kitchen work, household cleaning, and Morris dancing, I set up a station on the lawn to do charcoal caricatures of our guests for a small fee. Jon and another student, in a quick change to clown costumes, juggle. Late in the afternoon, the sun lowering in the sky, students and visitors join together in a huge circle-dance out on the lawn. Even the solemn manor house appears to bob up and down to the music.

Following dinner and cleanup, there is still more—the performance of Peer Gynt, a play about a man who runs away from being himself, refusing to evolve. Mr. Bennett causes a stir by playing the role of the Button Maker who melts down the souls of those who are neither good enough for heaven nor bad enough for hell.

Finally, the fête over, dinner finished, the performance of Peer Gynt complete, and all the company gone, Jonas follows me around the house talking at me non-stop as I'm putting away odds and ends, abandoned dishes, brooms, whatever I see out of place or undone. He speaks of Work philosophy, his experiences at Sherborne, his family, but no thought is complete. Nothing is making any sense to me. He rambles from one subject to another, incomprehensible. We've not spent that much time together lately and when we went on those exeats, I hadn't noticed anything like this. He's agitated in a way I've not seen before.

You can tell that he can't stop talking. He has no control over himself, and I'm exhausted, having never experienced anything this frantic. Finally, I just stand there, bewildered.

"I can't bear this," I tell him, "and I don't know how to put an end to it."

"My mother said the same thing to my father," Jonas says. "Maybe we'll be lucky. At least we won't have eleven kids like they do—well, maybe not lucky, just different."

I'm thinking, When had we discussed marriage?

I am so tired my eyes are closing even as I'm standing there with him. He suggests we sleep outside. Fresh air sounds good, and the instant we crawl into the sleeping bag I drift off. But he soon awakens me, wanting to make love.

"I have too much energy," he says.

We make love and I fall asleep again. Then he awakens me a second time.

"I'm uncomfortable in this small bag," he tells me. As soon as he's quiet, I fall back to sleep, but he awakens me again.

"I think I'll go in."

"Okay," I say with my eyes still closed, then struggle to stand up, blissful over the thought of going to my luxurious cot.

He stops walking and says, "I think I'll go in alone."

I'm not supposed to walk to the house with him? "What are you up to?" I sputter, now wide-awake.

"Talk is my failure," he says and then walks off. After a few minutes of collecting my befuddled self, taking deep breaths under the starry sky, I trudge to the entrance. Jonas is standing inside the doorway waiting for me. I should just walk by, but I stop and look up at him, hoping for clarity. Whatever it is he's saying, I finally understand that something is seriously wrong with him. He goes off to his room and I go to mine.

A glance out the window shows the sky beginning to lighten. My God! This had been going on all night. What can be done? Can anyone *here* help him? I've watched this happen

to others during the year. I'm so disturbed by his mental condition, I'm afraid to go to sleep only to awaken later more deeply
immersed in sorrow. But this is Sherborne. I'll sleep for a few
hours, and life will continue. I'll still be trying to assess whether
this place is operating on some wise engine of persistence-in-
the-face-of-difficulty or plain old insanity.

28 ∾ BEGINNING OF THE END

*The very aim of our society seems to be to remove from
people responsibility for their lives and acts. The way of
transformation must be the exact opposite of this.*

JG Bennett

In late June, after the fête, Mr. B announces that a Cambodian
Buddhist monk he calls Bhanté, or Grandfather, will be joining
us. When traveling in India, Mick had met Bhanté and studied
with him at his ashram. Upon his return to England, Mick told
Mr. B about Bhanté's teachings. After appearing to Mr. B during
a meditation, he invited the old monk to come to Sherborne to
teach his specialty—color meditation.

Bhanté is a stocky eighty-six-year-old man with a shaved
head and skin that glows like strong tea. He wears either the traditional burgundy or saffron robes, saturated colors that bring
comfort to my eyes. We students follow a little trail through ivy
and woods to another out-building where we painted a room
green for the healing meditations that Bhanté shares with us.

Many of the students find sitting in the deep green room lit with a green flood light soothing. Although I love the green of nature, I find the artificial lighting claustrophobic and dark. The more sessions I attend, the more irritable I become.

"You are just experiencing a cleansing phase," Bhanté assures me, but the phase never ends. My need for cleansing must be far greater than he anticipated. Despite my bad temper, hearing what Bhanté says is a balm. Even in his broken English, his meaning is clear. He begins or ends each meditation by reminding us to hold thoughts of goodwill and loving kindness for all sentient beings.

In one lecture, he speaks of five hindrances to spiritual life—unrestrained sensuous desire, ill will, sloth, worry and restlessness, and skeptical thinking. These are easy to recognize compared to the foreign vocabulary used by Mr. B. I revel in the simplicity.

My generous food-sharing roommate Bev, with the dark curls, is also enthralled with Bhanté. He invites us to join him in the morning before Morning Exercise for an additional regimen of physical exercise and lessons about what he refers to as the colored waters and oils he uses for healing. Each morning I make note of what he tells us and am awed by Bhanté's physical flexibility that, even at eighty-six easily surpasses mine.

It isn't the waters that are actually colored; it's the glass bottles in which the water is stored. Bhanté instructs us for using the most common colored bottles, green and brown. He has other colors, too, orange, blue, and yellow, all prepared by exposing the oil or water-filled bottles to sunlight out on the roof. The oil he uses is sunflower seed oil, but most bottles are filled with water.

He tells us not to fill the bottles higher than where the glass begins to curve. One day of bright sun is enough, certainly no more than a week. We should stand the bottles a bottle-width apart and when we bring them inside, keep them in the dark or wrap them in foil. He shows us to use green water by applying it to an injury with a piece of soaked cotton or by having the patient take it internally.

"Green water," he says, "is for reducing fever, healing injuries, or to stop bleeding, pain, and eczema. It also cures loose bowel movements. Green oil is applied to old wounds that continue to ooze."

He uses brown water for liver ailments, to improve circulation, and to cure constipation and arrested menstrual periods.

My interest in all kinds of alternative medicine already introduced me to the idea of color for its psychological effects, but I haven't heard of using color for physical conditions. I'm somewhat skeptical but I'm also familiar with the placebo effect that provides as good a percentage of improvement as what a pharmaceutical medicine needs in order to be considered statistically significant. Bev and I also spend time with him when students seek help for many of the conditions already mentioned, and we see some good results.

An idea begins to brew in my mind about setting up a meditation workshop for Bhanté to teach at the Edgar Cayce Foundation. A house there could accommodate students for the duration of a residential workshop. Although I previously harbored notions about moving to California when I return to the States, such thoughts drift further away while images of Virginia Beach take hold. For the first time since I've been at Sherborne I am thinking of the future.

Two young men traveled with Bhanté to Sherborne. One is a Western acolyte with a shaven head who wears a saffron robe. He is Bhanté's assistant, always accompanying him and running countless errands. At first, Bhanté conveys the impression that his helper might be incompetent, but over time I see that Bhanté is quite the taskmaster in contrast to his docile manner.

The other companion is a rugged red-haired Irishman named Emmett, coincidentally from Chicago. His curly hair and blue eyes don't prevent him from transmitting the intense demeanor of a Turk. He joins in the activities of the course as if he's been there all along. Our paths keep crossing during the day until we come to take zealous walks together during tea or lunch breaks. It's a needed respite from dealing with Jonas with whom I still spend small amounts of time at greater intervals.

Emmett has the gift of being fully involved in anything he participates in while not being at all attached to it. He entertains me with stories about his recent experiences in India. Before he met Bhanté, he hiked alone in the cool mountains of India and became very ill, apparently passing a kidney stone. He went through this ailment all alone, running a high fever and in so much pain, helpless to move. After three days of lying on the ground, when he recovered and was able to walk again, he came down into a city near Bhanté's enclave. As he wandered the streets, he thought he'd lost his mind or perhaps was still sicker than he realized. Compared to the mountains, it felt warm there, in the high seventies. But groups of people huddled around fire barrels where they stood rubbing their hands to keep warm. Later, he learned that the normal daytime temperatures usually reached one hundred and twenty degrees, and when it dropped to the seventies, people were really cold.

During a silent work period on the grounds, I notice Emmett stationed at the tall hedges. At the end of the day, when I walk past the bushes, he is about to load his high mound of weeds into the wheelbarrow. Still carrying my garden fork, I join him without words to hoist the stack. I'll miss these simple interactions with him when he and Bhanté's entourage soon leave.

It is the second week of July, and Bhanté makes his farewell speech. Mr. Bennett thanks him and says we will continue the green meditations, but I can't imagine them being the same without Bhanté's colorful presence and gentle prayers.

On the same day, Jonas confesses to me that he's been sick for weeks; yet he refuses to see anyone about it. He talks of it as if it were a physical illness but his refusal to seek help makes me think he suspects it's something more. Though we're not spending much time together, our discussion is civil yet distant.

Meditation has become a greater part of the program than ever before. In Morning Exercise I still speak my usual inner mantra: I'm cold and my back hurts. Then I wonder, where the hell am I in sensing my limbs? Which one am I on? I've lost my place. If I hold a Russian prayer in my heart, I forget the English one in my head. Have I counted my breaths or differentiated the strength of each latifa? Maybe a little nap is all I really need.

On good days, I remember to start all over again. In hopeful moments, I think I can sit for one more forty-five minute exercise—a tentative commitment.

Sometimes, the words of the Work enthusiasts come to mind. Occasionally one or another seeks me out uninvited to let me know that I am one of the people leaking vital group energy instead of contributing to it, by laughing or by having a boyfriend. They never seek me out to confess anything about their own contributions to the situation, which can be observed as easily as mine.

In our meditations, I often have the sensation of sitting to the left of myself, as if I were "beside myself." In an uncharacteristic stroke of student-ness, I tell Mr. B about it.

"Don't worry," he says. "Sit next to me tonight. I'll help you."

I sit beside him, settling in like a rock, quiet for the first time in a long stretch. A few days later I tell Bev what happened, and she asks me what he did. I have no idea, nor do I go back and ask him. Meditations continue to remain less agitated, though never as peaceful as I imagine they are supposed to be.

With the conclusion of the fête and Bhanté's leaving, Mr. Bennett calls many meetings to concentrate on solidifying what we will be taking away from Sherborne and how we might share what we have learned with others. We make lists of Work concepts and then of tasks that can be done each week with a Work group we might lead. The tasks have the flavor of themes for self-observation but feel smaller in their scope, perhaps more in scale with our understanding. I make notes and wonder if I'll ever create a situation in which to make use of them.

As disconnected as I feel toward the Work as it is presented to us here, I do appreciate methods of self-observation; practical work; Theme; learning to recognize functioning of the head, emotional, and moving centers; and the benefits of community tasks and shared silence. I can imagine some situations where it would make sense to share some of what I learned. My internal conflict with Work language isn't so important when I focus on the experiences.

To add to a growing sense of completion, in the second week of July I finish tiling the fireplace! Concluding the task when I thought I had failed is a little like thinking my diet permanently ruined after eating some gooey dessert. I learn that I can pick up where I've left off and do not have to give up.

The air is crackling with everyone's anticipation of leaving Sherborne within a month. After a brisk Movements class, Wade, from the Morris team, jokes with me. He always seems to be in good humor. He's one of the contingent of students who had come from California together. Tonight he suggests we step outside for some fresh air. Standing close to the front door, he invites me to walk with him to another village.

"It's past 10:00 p.m.," I answer while looking into his beaming smile. I am a little surprised that someone who usually seems so sensible is thinking of going for a hike at this hour.

"Sure, we could go to Northleach."

"Northleach?" I echo. "That's five miles from here."

"There's a little caff there, and it's open late for lorry drivers."

He pronounces café 'caff' like the English do, then grins about his little between-us-Americans' joke.

"C'mon, let's try it. We can always stop walking if it feels too far." His straight white teeth make his smile glow in the dark like the Cheshire cat's.

"Okay . . . why not?"

For a couple of weeks, we amaze ourselves by walking to Northleach and back almost every night after Movements class, an easy amble with all the energy we've accumulated from the activities of the course. As much as I complain about every moment being filled with doing something, my physical energy level has never been higher in my entire life. I've always enjoyed walking, but Wade tells me that walking and talking for hours are high on his 'unlikely' scale. We must be processing the whole Sherborne experience. That's all we talk about.

On one of the last visitors' weekends, Les and Selene, an Australian couple, lead the kitchen crew in making fresh peach ice cream by hand, each of us taking turns crushing the ice crystals with a wooden paddle. Any kind of ice cream is a treat, but making it ourselves without machinery causes a flurry of mouth watering anticipation.

Before we can no longer be tourists in Great Britain, Wade and I take advantage of the next exeat to go to Minster Lovell, the ruins of Richard III's henchman, Lord Lovell. We hitch a ride on the motorway east to Witney where we delight in bumping into Dallas, as if he were a long lost friend, and the three of us revel in spending an easygoing day together filled with the promise of a future far from Sherborne. From Witney, we walk a few miles northwest to the ruins, our eyes fed by sunshine and spring green grass around and inside the jagged stone vestiges, the lush growth reflecting our growing sense of a fast approaching future. The remains of the fifteenth century manor house consists of a foundation that is barely the outline of a hall and tower, while a classic beehive shaped dovecote nearby stands complete and beautiful. We bend down to enter through a low doorway. Inside, the ghosts of birds fluttering between dome and nesting boxes fill the emptiness, and sunlight pours down from the open clerestory at the apex, giving a soft glow to the rhythmic symmetrical interior.

Knowing it is too late to catch a bus to arrive at Sherborne in time for dinner, we decide to hitchhike and eat out along the way. In order to find drivers willing to pick up all three of us, we decide it is essential to look as harmless as possible. Lining up in order of height at the edge of the road, we send out our most friendly smiles and put our synchronized Movements skills to practice, coordinating posture and thumbing gestures. We soon get a ride to Burford, another to an inn where we dine, and from there a third and final trip right to Sherborne's front door.

It is still July when I launch my grand chocolate cure. I hear that one of the students resolved his ice cream addiction by overeating it and then throwing up. Knowing my appetite for chocolate, I doubt I would ever get sick from it. The most I can hope for, with any luck, is to get good and tired of the taste for the long term.

I cut classes this afternoon with the purpose of executing my recovery. At the Post Office, I purchase a large chocolate roll, a one-pound fruit and nut bar, three 3/4 oz. bars of chocolate with peanuts, two Marathon bars, and a large Toblerone, thinking the variety will allow me to consume more. I escort my prizes past the white cockatoo who greets all passersby from one of the village garden walls. Nearby I enter the shortcut through the woods to find a good spot where I can concentrate on eating. The smaller candy bars go down easily. After the one-pounder, the chocolate has as much flavor as cardboard—a good sign, I tell myself. No more sparkle of mouth-watering sugar and chocolate. I'm slowing down, but stalwart, continuing to chew away. I don't feel ill, but I can't consume the last two tasteless pieces of Toblerone so I stick them in my pocket.

Something beyond tastelessness is happening. Something is making me sing aloud as I totter back to school. It is in my mind to visit Gertie and ask her if she thinks I've eaten enough to accomplish my aim. On my way, I bump into Jonas, who unpredictable as ever, greets me this time with a warm hug. I moan a salutation into his chest as the image of all I've consumed floats through my mind to the accompaniment of rumbling intestines. Suddenly, I feel it imperative to finish the last two pieces. I must complete this worthy project! Tearing myself away, I rush to the loo to finish the job in private, resisting all temptation to tell Jonas or anyone I pass in the halls about my grand feat. Yes, I am thinking something like, 'May the energy raised by my work be transubstantiated within me.'

It is the next day, and I regard it a miracle that I don't have a hangover. I am feeling fine, on house duty, and hurrying to my assignment when I pass my friend Lucas moving just as hurriedly in the opposite direction.

"Here's something for you," he says, grabbing my hand and closing my fingers around a small object as he rushes off down the hall. I open my hand to see what he's given me. A nice chunk of Cadbury Chocolate Fruit and Nut. I eagerly toss it into my mouth witho ₍ a moment's hesitation. Mmmmm! Delicious!

Too much of a good thing is wonderful.

Mae West

29 ᴥ PREPARING TO LEAVE

Your work will hold together if you all struggle for your own being. Then you will be able to profit by what comes to you from outside. Also you will learn how to use for your own being all the vicissitudes of your practical everyday life.

JG Bennett

For several weeks I've been helping the people who wish to be Movements instructors make notes of the Movements. I enjoy developing a shorthand visual language of stick figures representing all the different positions each file performs.

Yet another of the end-of-the-course projects that we all participate in is for each of us to lead a Movements class. I dread having to lead a class, but right away I think of a Movement that has an interesting pattern of the gestures shifting from one file to the next. I am curious to see how this feels to do it in a circle with the six files facing a center rather than in the usual block formation of files and rows with everyone facing forward. After class, I hear some rumblings about my creative endeavor as students leave, but I don't give them a second thought. I'm glad the class is over with.

When I come out of Morning Exercise the following day, I am accosted, moments apart by several teachers telling me in one way or another that my egotistic experiment has caused a commotion. Each one reprimands me for taking the liberty of changing the form of a Movement.

"You do not know what you are doing." "You are not in any position to make such a decision." The fact that the news is traveling at all takes me by surprise. I hadn't intended to change a Movement for all posterity. I wasn't even planning to teach Movements. I was merely curious. At mid-day, Mick, too, who's heard about my transgression, is animated as he tells me, while chuckling, that he has seen the Movement done exactly that way in the Middle East as part of a Dervish ceremony.

"It's obvious you sensed the original formation," he says, and I enjoy his confirming my intuition.

At another meeting, Mr. B points to the different perceptions of men and women.

"In terms of mesoteric activities, women have a stronger perception of 'now' and men have a stronger perception of 'future possibilities.' In the esoteric world," he says, "men and women are the same in their perceptions."

As students, we've come to appreciate, throughout the course, some of the inherent differences in how men and women approach ordinary physical tasks and interactions. The women are more sensitive to details—the relevance of fine points in all subjects including people; men are more physical and motivated by the big picture. These differences of perception come up in everything from washing dishes to involvement with the children. Even the style of gardening we've developed reflect our male and female discernment. For example, one often sees in the garden how the women sit on the ground to pick the weeds out of the loosened soil, while the men, taking no note of the weeds left behind, dig up the entire plot in no time, turning over large clumps of earth and moving on as fast as they can. If the women don't pick the weeds out, they will be left there to continue growing. But the men cover a lot of ground and get the whole plot turned over. There are benefits to both of our perceptions.

Mr. B speaks to us about sex again, celibacy in particular.

"What a terrible loss, " he says. "It may have been one of the most destructive acts of the Church to require that people who had the strongest sense of spirituality become celibate."

CELIBACY IS NOT HEREDITARY.

Anonymous

Questions regarding the subject of polygamy come up because many of our meditative exercises, Movements, and ablutions are derived from Islamic tradition and, perhaps, even more ancient practices originating in the Caucasus. Mr. B speaks of three conditions for the man to meet in order for polygamy to work well:

1. Adequate material provision
2. Virility to satisfy more than one woman
3. Enough authority to be accepted by more than one

He also says that having sex affects one much more deeply than people realize.

"Intercourse is an essence act—something is taken from the participants even if the personality forgets. If one wants to become free, this makes for difficulties. One pays a price. A woman's perception becomes unreliable. We see this in her inability to perceive a man's temperament. Men, on the other hand, will find it difficult to develop awareness."

In the new era of free sex, I have experienced and see the recognizable consequences all around me. Women fall in love with their fantasies of the men they know, paying little attention to their actual behaviors and attitudes until deep into the relationship; and men remain childish in how they respond to people and situations.

Mr. B also gives some guidelines for life after the Sherborne course ends in mid-August. He reminds us as he had when we first arrived, "Don't read a lot, especially for the first few months after leaving." Perhaps he wants us to take time to absorb our experiences and continue practicing some of the exercises before straying too far from them with distractions from outside. He also suggests that Morning Exercise be done at least once a week with others, though it needn't be done in the morning and shouldn't be done in a room painted and lit for Bhanté's green meditation.

Mr. B makes a number of comments about Zikr. He recommends that we do not do it for more than an hour at a time and to include the holding of breath. He reminds us that when our Work has gone sour, practicing Zikr during the day for three days is a valuable way to get back on track.

"Do it for a minute or two out of each hour and include breath holding." He says that fasting and Zikr go well together, and if you can't fast for health reasons "it can be profitable to skip a meal on occasion and do the Zikr during that time instead."

I note everything mostly with detachment. Nothing seems to pull at me any more. Yet when he suggests we revisit the religion of our birth, something in me perks up.

"Just see if you can understand it differently now."

I plan on doing that.

More question and answer meetings with Mr. B gives us a last opportunity to hear what he has been trying to convey all year and ease our transition back into the world. We sit in the downstairs library, almost always the place for these meetings. The drought this summer means that sunlight is streaming in the windows, a stark contrast to the dark dreary light of our long winter.

One question stands out: "This Work seems so dismal," a student says. "Isn't there any room for humor and play?"

Mr. Bennett sits for a long time, appearing to look deep within. Then he raises his eyes to the questioner and smiles.

"How could God have made butterflies if we were to be without cheer?" he answers.

I sigh. The course could benefit from a lot more butterflies. I seek their equivalent almost always outside of class except in this last third of the year when our activities accommodated more creativity and Morris dance play. Creativity doesn't seem subject to the constant stream of analysis that plagues the world of thought and observation.

Another question is whether Mr. B notes any effect on the children who grew up in a Work community that is different from children raised in ordinary circumstances.

He answers, "There is one quality I consistently notice. The children who grow up in places such as Coomb Springs are much more tolerant toward others. They have met so many different types of people and interacted with them, even if only in play."

He describes how they learn, as we have, that people have many sides to them. A person might be both annoying and a great partner to have fun with; an unusual looking person could be compassionate; a distant person might only be shy; and when their parents are too busy, there is always someone around who responds to them. They're comfortable speaking with adults, can look them in the eye, and expect to take part in conversations.

A young man asks if Mr. B intends to have another community like Coombe Springs when he finishes the Sherborne project. Mr. B looks surprised, then laughs, as if the question is a joke, "Oh, no. I don't intend to live in a community ever again." Why is he teaching us all these community-oriented ways? Or did he have a premonition there'd be no time for him to live in a community after Sherborne?

We rarely have to wait any more through long tense silences before someone else speaks.

"Why should we work so hard?" another student asks.

Mr. Bennett looks down into his hands as he folds them. A long silence passes as he thinks about his answer. When he finally looks up he says, "So we can bear more."

This time the room *is* quiet for a long time while we contemplate the answer.

I feel sure he is right, yet in life outside of Sherborne, I know so many harried and unhappy people who work hard and who say yes to everything without discrimination. We won't be able to do everything. Should we be able to do everything that crosses our paths? Will we be able to do more yet recognize the right courses of action?

Another question is asked. "Why can't Man accomplish what he knows how to do?"

"Man is capable of many great achievements. He has physical resources and knowledge. It is his being asleep about his true nature that gets in the way. Man does not yet understand enough about himself. Imagine what could be accomplished if he didn't demand personal recognition and power over others."

Ah, that again. How our egos get in the way of what we know and could accomplish.

ACCOMPLISHING THE IMPOSSIBLE MEANS ONLY THAT
THE BOSS WILL ADD IT TO YOUR REGULAR DUTIES.

Doug Larson

Mr. B has been leading green meditations since Bhanté left. I still find them disturbing. At the most recent one, I become even more agitated than usual, unable to listen to Mr. B using Bhanté's words. I cannot sit still, so I stand quietly and am surprised to see that perhaps a third of the other students are doing the same thing. We leave to silently follow the path through ivy and woods back to the house. Later, someone who stayed tells me that Mr. B continued with the meditation saying, "Now that only those who should be here are here, we can get on with it." As the course winds down, Warren and Lucia, his girl friend, break up. Through the diet and physical work, puffy nondescript Warren had gotten muscular. His skin has become clear and he looks quite handsome. Lucia, on the other hand, has retreated. Has her state contributed to their breaking up or is it the other way around?

Her black pixie style hair, dark somber eyes, and a strong Southern accent should convey sensuality but, instead, she's brittle. Had she always been this way? I hadn't noticed her much before the breakup. Her behavior has grown so odd I wonder if she is reachable. I hope Mr. Bennett knows what's best for her.

From anywhere in the building, at unexpected moments throughout the day I hear her yell like a Kung Fu master, "No!" When I happen to be nearby, I can't see that her cry is apropos of anything happening outwardly. I want to say something but can think of nothing, not even a few words of sympathy. Mr. B must perceive my inner agreement with her for on several recent occasions when he passes me in the hall, he greets me with, "Hello, Lucia."

Even with the anticipation of leaving and, the now more affirming light mood, aside from what I see in Lucia, I am enthusiastic to apply to my life what I learned about creating energy and making more useful self-observations. However, while I agree with the intent and activities of the school, the harsh attitudes still feel unbalanced and leave me ambivalent.

I have a sense that my fellow-Sherbornites are people with whom I had a long history before this lifetime. All I can do is wait to see what the future reveals. Will our paths cross again and where will my work bring me?

I can't help but think of Mr. B as a godparent in the most traditional sense of the word. He is the first person to mentor me about spiritual matters in a practical way; and when we speak with each other about the exercises, I feel the importance of his sharing years of practice while he conveys respect for my experiences and yearnings, even as he calls me by the wrong name.

I MAY NOT HAVE GONE WHERE I INTENDED TO GO,
BUT I THINK I HAVE ENDED UP WHERE I INTENDED TO BE.

Douglas Adams

30 ❧ IS THERE LIFE
AFTER SHERBORNE?

*You see, the truth is that nothing is real so long as
our inside and our outside are separated from one
another.*

JG Bennett

August 15, 1973 and the course at Sherborne House is officially completed. As a grand finale to our time in England, Guy and Veronica, the older couple Jonas and I visited to enjoy their garden and build a bookshelf, invites us to join them touring the northern canals in a houseboat for twelve days. Jonas seems to have come through the crisis he had during the fête. We are settled into a platonic mostly cordial truce. I welcome the opportunity to decompress from the rigors of Sherborne and spend neutral time with Jonas in the company of other people.

Before meeting with Guy and Veronica, we go with Betty and Morgan for a few days to their home up in Birmingham. We help them unpack the household goods that have been in storage. Jonas and Morgan will spend a couple of days moving furniture from garage to house while Betty and I organize the kitchen and closets.

The first carton we open is labeled Large Cooking Pots. We pull up the flaps and peer in. Compared to the cooking vessels of Sherborne in which we prepared meals for a hundred, these pots appear to be children's toys. I pick up a two-liter teakettle holding my pinkie in the air.

In a squeaky voice, I say, "Look at this wee kettle."

Betty says, "Could I possibly have given the whole family tea from that?"

Then Betty dangles the largest stew pot from her index finger.

"Look at this! A miniature cauldron."

We repeat variations on this joke a dozen times throughout the day, laughing every time. Later in the day, the idea comes up in our conversation: Perhaps these aren't the only things distorted by our year at Sherborne!

From Birmingham, Jonas and I, along with Betty and Morgan's eleven-year-old son, Jay, meet up with Guy and Veronica. They generously pay the greater share toward renting the houseboat we pilot through the North Country canals. Jay travels by boat with us for little more than a day until his parents pick him up in a nearby town. Although Jonas pays little attention to me, I'm overjoyed to be laughing and chatting with Veronica.

She regales us with stories about her studies with Mr. Bennett over the past thirty years, awakening in the middle of the night, driven to completing an unfinished Decision Exercise while practically sleepwalking. She tells of garden experiments she and Guy conduct in their conservative suburban surroundings. They sneak out in the middle of the night to urinate 'al fresco' on the compost heap. It feels good to laugh and take note of how they've melded their life and humor with the Work.

In Sheffield, Jonas and I take a bus to pick up our classmate Malcolm, who Betty, Patrick, and I had teased about not understanding his accent in our early days of Sherborne. He's going to travel with us on the houseboat for three days. Just as Malcolm described many months ago, we can barely understand what anyone is saying out on the streets, their accent so different. The North Atlantic colors of York also contrast with the Cotswolds. Instead of cream-colored stone buildings, the houses here are a dark red brick. The Cotswold, almost chartreuse, green is replaced with a forest green of the North Country. The deep saturated colors of a new landscape are refreshing.

The boat has bunks for six and a complete kitchen. We chug along the canal, taking in pastoral panoramas. When we spot a farmhouse, we moor the boat so Veronica and I can hike across the field to purchase fresh milk and eggs directly from the farmer's wife. Whenever we see an exceptional spot at the side of the canal, we stop to have our next meal or moor for the night so we can enjoy the view again in the morning. It's delicious to be following our inner rhythms and not an imposed schedule.

Veronica shows me an easy way to make yogurt, placing the jar of heated milk and culture in a warmed turned-off oven so it will cool slowly overnight with plenty of time to grow; she also bakes bread each day. Together we cook most of our meals right here in the galley. With no demands put on us, life is simple.

We have been given a huge old key—like something out of a fairy tale—to open and close the locks of the canals. The routine is to navigate right up to the front lock gates, secure the second set of gates behind us, then allow the water to rise or fall as needed. Then we open the first set and cruise on through. This repetitive action is almost meditative. One time, there is actually a lock keeper who lives in the nearby lock house. He, too, looks like a character in a fairy tale, brawny and with a full beard, the magical woodsman. He tells us about the dwindling need for lockkeepers and how, with cutbacks, he now watches over several locks. Together we mourn the changing way of life.

Only once do we moor near a city—Leeds. We spend the night outside of town, far enough away for quiet and close enough to arrive early in the morning. Veronica has arranged the whole day. She is intent on visiting the Pennines, a rounded mountain range extending from the Scottish border about half-way down through England. She's talked about it ever since we set out. In town we take a motor coach that lets us off at the bottom of gently sloping mountains. I walk with Veronica whose bubbling personality makes it easy to enjoy the misty rain. Pale gray rock outcroppings are everywhere; brilliant green grass is soaked by the gentle drizzle and nibbled by sheep until it looks like velvet. The cloud cover, thin as tissue paper, lets in a sooth-ing light that glows pale blueness in every direction. Unlike an American park in the rain, the hills are animated with people, whole families with their children dressed like clones of Pad-dington Bear, all wearing electric yellow slickers and red rubber boots. They pass us going in every direction, and it feels as if we are walking through an illustration in a children's book.

We keep walking upward until we see spread below us a valley from left to right. Maybe it's as much as a mile long, filled with what I guess to be hundreds of sheep. While they are graz-ing, a single sheepdog takes obvious pleasure in keeping the flock together by running the full length of the valley, from one end of the flock to the other. I relish the freedom to walk at lei-sure and breathe in this unique scene.

The next day we deliver Malcolm back to York and complete our journey on the canal. Jonas and I spend another couple of days with Guy and Veronica at their home surrounded by the bursting garden. It is exactly a year from when I arrived at Sherborne. Now I know what it takes to create a harvest like this. I also know something more about myself.

Still, there are plenty more questions about who I can become, what the course at Sherborne will mean in the future. Will I retain the practices that seem to provide a more concrete way of expressing spiritual life, meditation and sensing that bring me to an internal quiet place, an expanded view of the present moment that makes me more patient about what I perceive of people and situations?

Being with Guy and Veronica is a perfect transition between the unusual school and my life in the world. Jonas and I know we aren't going to be seeing each other anymore. We fly to New York where we say our good-byes, feeling no regrets, just a quiet bittersweet sentiment on my part. I take a last look at his boyish dishevelment, a fresh feather in the buttonhole of his shirt, his saddle shoes. We turn our backs to each other and amble off to our respective destinations.

On the plane I am immersed in a flurry of thoughts—both relief and anticipation. I am already sure that Sherborne has been a life-changing event, a greatly enhanced experience just because choosing to be there was not a legal educational directive nor imposed by family expectations. Neither were we rewarded in any of the ways our culture usually rewards education with diplomas or grants, promises of employment or letters after our names. Making efforts corresponded to our own understanding. We assessed the results guided by our intentions. It was an opportunity rarely experienced in the lives we live outside of Sherborne. Imagine if students could participate in their schooling by setting their own goals and being taught how to achieve them through decision-making and the expectation of lifelong continuous education. It would revolutionize our culture.

However, I still quake over feeling stifled by the predictable, narrow, and humorless understanding of emotions. The feeling atmosphere is something I will still have to sort out. I've learned a little about the difference between putting pressure on oneself and having it brought to bear by others. Without a clear sense of one's own boundaries, and a lack of perception about other people, pressure from the outside can easily slip into abuse.

I worry about several students who couldn't bear Sherborne, Ivo who left at the beginning and two others who had to leave mid-year. Will Jonas be okay? And what about Lucia who seemed to have a breakdown, shouting "No" into the empty halls? Did she receive any help? And these are the students whose mental states I'm aware of.

IT IS A BIT EMBARRASSING TO HAVE BEEN CONCERNED WITH
THE HUMAN PROBLEM ALL ONE'S LIFE AND FIND AT THE END
THAT ONE HAS NO MORE TO OFFER BY WAY OF ADVICE THAN
"TRY TO BE A LITTLE KINDER."

Aldous Huxley

The stewardess distracts me from my reverie as she hands me a glass of water. Yet I quickly drift into images of Sherborne again, this time returning to the day the course was officially over, the building once again jangling with chaotic vibes just like when we were all arriving—my lonely entrance, other new arrivals daily, feeling all the anxiety hanging in the air about what the future holds.

Some of my fellow students left at the instant they could, and despite the building being half empty, there was frenetic movement in the air. Those of us still there were busy organizing ourselves, mailing packages home in order to travel lighter, making plans to be tourists before heading back to the States or other countries. Others were getting themselves settled in to work on the two-month transition before the third class arrives while a few were planning to take a break before becoming staff for the third course.

I visited the ground floor room into which we were dumping boots and clothing we no longer wanted. Standing on the periphery of piles of cast-offs along with three other students, I recognized a too-well-known bathrobe as having belonged to Tomás. We entered into a spontaneous litany.

"Ooooh, look! It's Tomás," I call out, while holding the blue robe up for them to see.

"Oh, yeah. That's his."

For five minutes, each of us took a turn holding some item of clothing aloft and toasting the classmate who left it behind.

"Isn't this Rene's red hooded sweatshirt?"

"Uh huh. Rene's!" we responded.

"Dallas's blue jumper!"

"Dallas's blue jumper!" we echoed.

I hoped to find Colette's fur boots or Toby's black cape, but no such treasures surfaced. It crossed my mind to squirrel away all recognizable items as mementos for a stuffed-trunk scrapbook, but thankfully the idea slipped away before it crystallized. Instead, we all stood there together, savoring the last sighting of each item displayed.

I couldn't resist appropriating Terrie's cotton T-shirt, softened to the consistency of cheesecloth from innumerable washings. I loved the reminder-of-spring lilac color. I could even consider wearing the scoop neck style now that I wouldn't be freezing to death. That fact, in itself, was a cheery harbinger of a new life ahead.

After our group liturgy of premature nostalgia, on the way to my room, I passed through the upstairs hall near men's dorm room 10. Mr. Bennett was walking toward me from the direction of his apartment. There were no convenient stairwells to duck into. I looked for a door to dart behind. Why did I want to avoid him? No time to give it more thought. With his long strides, he reached me in a split second, grasped my upper arms, and gave me a big kiss on the lips.

"You're a genius," he bellowed, looking me in the eyes. "Those tiles! A genius!"

Flabbergasted by his enthusiasm, all I could do, in the spirits of Lucia and myself, was shriek.

"Noooooo!"

To which he said nothing. As he walked on his way, I imagined him shaking his head in amused resignation.

I know I was shaking mine.

∾

In memoriam
John Godolphin Bennett
June 8, 1897–December 13, 1974

Also by BJ Appelgren

The Transparent Feather

Berry Morgan, a regular contributor to *The New Yorker* magazine, is living out her days in a nursing home. She works out a unique partnership with an aspiring writer—BJ Appelgren will transcribe Berry's memoirs, and in return Berry will help develop BJ's writing.

The unanticipated laughter and friendship at a critical time in both women's lives takes them by surprise. While Berry makes peace with her own life, she hands over the joy she feels for the process of writing, cheering BJ on as the novice stumbles to find her writing voice and meet life's challenges.

"*The Transparent Feather* is a many-layered book full of rich color and marvelous descriptions. It has universal appeal."

Mary Lehman, editor, *The Shepherdstown Observer*

". . . as Berry's story faded and failed, the author's grew stronger and took her place. There was a sublime and touching passing of the order and also revealed the authentic exploration of the writing process."

Robert Dixon Bell, history teacher

"This is an inspiring tale of a serendipitous friendship leading to growth and self-revelation."

Joyce Lerner, book designer

"BJ and Berry quietly shared the everydayness of time slipping on, both knowing Berry was dying. As a clinician and psychotherapist, I know others need it—a non-gendered spiritually committed version of *Tuesdays With Morrie.*"

Dr. Heidi Spencer, psychotherapist

". . . a complex work, immediately rewarding as the story of a new found passion and unexpected friendship—the elegantly awkward exchange of vitality between one human being and another. As one door closes, another opens. In it's depths, however, one is invited to an eclectic meditation on the many forms of "parenting." In particular, that grave yet pregnant moment, in the long slow dance of parent and child, teacher and student, when familiar roles reverse—challenging each to embrace, or resist, the intimation that death is calling the changes."

Stephen Longworth, psychotherapist

Available at Amazon and wherever fine books are sold by special order or as e-books. Print: ISBN 0-9619884-0-1 $14.95